MW00974436

A Passion for Christ

A Passion for Souls

Encouragements for the Day

◆

Spirit-filled Inspirations for Every Day

Kwesi R. Kamau

XULON PRESS

To Aunt Evelyn

Thank you so much
for leading me,
guiding me, supporting
me and more
importantly loving
me as a niece
and a sister
in Christ.
Bless you,
Love You
Diana
Xmas 03

Dedication

◆

To My Wife and Beautiful Children

Foreword

◆

A Passion for Christ, A Passion for Souls: Encouragements for the Day is a collection of daily meditations prepared by Kwesi Kamau and offered to hundreds by electronic mail over the World Wide Web.

The encouragement messages began when a friend requested sermon tapes for encouragement while going through seminary. No tapes were available at the time, but Kamau began writing down some thoughts from his devotional meditations and sending them instead. He decided to send them to a few other friends as well.

What started as a friendly exchange between Kamau and a few friends became a refreshing ministry to uncounted hundreds of people around the world. This collection comprises some favorites from over a three year period of daily encouragements. May these messages bless and refresh your walk with the Lord and enliven within you a passion for Christ and for souls.

Spirit-filled Inspirations
for Every Day

Time for a Change

And God raised us up with Christ and seated us with him in the heavenly realms in Christ Jesus. —Ephesians 2:6

A new year always brings a sense of new beginnings. People set so-called "New Year's resolutions." Fiscal years close and open. Seasons recycle. During the customary time off, we all have time to, as the Bible says, "consider our ways" and to catch our breath for a new start in our lives. The coming of a new year is a special time. It is a time for change.

As we take on this new year, we should focus on laying a new foundation in our lives. Take a good look and the things on which you are basing your life. Examine what is really important to you. Is it your business? Is it your family? Your position? Your relationship? Or is it really Christ and His Word?

Are you willing to make a real change? Are you willing to give up or lose what is really important to you to walk in the life God has for you? Can you sacrifice temporal things for an eternal weight of glory?

God has already raised us into new heights in the spirit, beloved. Still, to understand the joy and power of what God has prepared for us, we must be willing to let go of old trappings. It is time for a change. Let the Lord have His way and let this year be the best in your life.

Be encouraged.

Seize the Moment

"The Spirit of the Lord is on me, because he has anointed me to preach good news to the poor. He has sent me to proclaim freedom for the prisoners and recovery of sight for the blind, to release the oppressed, to proclaim the year of the Lord's favor." —Luke 4:18-19

This is the year of the Lord's favor. This year is to be the best year of your life as of yet. This is the year of tying good things together and breaking out of bad things. This is the year to claim a new level of maturity and to shed sins and habits that beset your spiritual progress. This is a year that has never been nor will ever be again.

Do not let this moment slip past you. You will face remorse if you do. Avoid looking back later this year with sorrow by rising to the occasion now and doing your best with each moment.

God has packed this year full of grace and you should go through it with great hopes. What do you want God to do for you? The time is now.

Fan the Flame

"Be not deceived, for God is not mocked; whatever a man sows, that shall he also reap." —Galatians 6:7

We must not think that we will grow in our fervor for the Lord not having sowed righteous seed in the Spirit. God has truly ordained for us to meditate on His word morning and evening (Ps. 1:2), to pray consistently (Eph. 6:18), to mourn and fast (Matt. 5:4), and to continue in all other good works (Gal. 6:10). He has for us to seek Him in worship and Bible Study and by any other means available.

I have truly seen, the more I commit to godly discipline and good works prescribed in the Bible, the hotter the fire of my soul gets. God wants us to do these things as much and even more than eating and drinking. It is utter foolishness to think one will taste of the divine fruit of revelation having sown so little in the endeavor.

I encourage you today to take every advantage to exercise godly discipline. Make it your first and most diligent employ. Seek first God's kingdom and righteousness and all other things will be added to you. (Matt. 6:33)

FAN THE FLAME!

A Passion for Souls

While Paul was waiting for them in Athens, he was greatly distressed to see that the city was full of idols. —Acts 17:16

Why is it so important to have a passion for souls?

Imagine your life without Christ. Just the notion of this is frightening. Think of the many things for which you have become dependant on Christ. When so many dread facing a new day, you have the promise of new mercies for the day. Everyone faces trials and troubles, yet you have faith to move mountains and a hope that will not disappoint. While anxiety grips our world, God's peace comes to still your soul.

These are but a few things. What others can you think of? Take a few moments and write down several ways you consciously depend on Christ each day. As you do this, also consider the soul around you that does not have Christ on which to lean. How does a person make it without him?

Stir up your spirit to rescue souls from darkness for the kingdom. Let us not be ashamed of the gospel, for it is the power of God unto salvation for everyone that believes!

Suffering and Truth

"I have told you these things, so that in me you may have peace. In this world you will have trouble. But take heart! I have overcome the world." —John 16:33

Good things do not come easy. One major problem in the modern day understanding of the church is that we expect things to come easy. We want a comfortable life without pain or suffering or struggle.

Struggles are a part of life. Suffering and pain is common to all men. Jesus says: "In this world you shall have trial and temptations, but be of good cheer, I have overcome the world." (John 16:33) We can debate the merits of pain and suffering in human existence, but this debate is pointless. Greater wisdom lies in realizing that they are real for every person and we must prepare ourselves for them as we are able.

Yet, since all will suffer, let us suffer doing what is right, good and profitable for the kingdom. Let God transform your pain into passion and your sorrow into strength.

Be encouraged.

Wisdom for the Ages

Let love and faithfulness never leave you; bind them around your neck, write them on the tablet of your heart. —Proverbs 3:3

How do you forge (or re-forge) a good reputation and a good name? Fill your life with kindness and loyalty toward others. The Bible says, "never let them leave you."

Sometimes the shadows of our mistakes and sins darken our hopes for change and growth in our lives. We ask ourselves, "how can I ever recover from this?" It is not easy. When our hearts condemn us, it is very hard to consider getting up and trying again. Yet every new day God gives a demonstration of His mercy. (Lam. 3:22-23)

Get up and try again. Do not let your failures rob you of your future successes. Every new day God gives you is a chance to walk away from your past. How do you start? Keep kindness and loyalty—love and faithfulness—with you, even when you do not *feel* it. They will obtain God's favor and the favor of those around you as well. (Prov. 3:4)

Be encouraged.

The Rest of God

"There remains, then, a Sabbath-rest for the people of God." —Hebrews 4:9

The Bible teaches us to "labor to enter into God's rest." There is a place in the Spirit that is wonderful, peaceful, blessed and powerfully dynamic all at once. There is an experience of God that is completely "addictive." There is a knowledge of undeniable victory and a sense of success through the recognition that all things are in God's hands. All of this abides in the rest of God.

When God finished creating and forming the heavens and the earth, He set a day for rest. We call this day the Sabbath and for thousands of years, the people of God distinguished themselves among the nations by recognizing the Sabbath and keeping it holy. Why was this done? Because God rested on this day and this had a very special significance. God's resting signified that all things are finished.

Indeed, as far as the God of eternity is concerned, all things are finished. God is not struggling with what He will do next or worried about how a certain thing will turn out. What is more wonderful is that God offers this assurance to us. He calls us close to Himself and through this passes His divine confidence to us.

Beloved, God is at rest and He wants us to enter into that rest. Let us assertively walk in the assurance that God has already worked out what we need for this day. Labor to do so and be encouraged.

Laboring for the Rest

Let us, therefore, make every effort to enter that rest, so that no one will fall by follow-ing their example of disobedience.
—Hebrews 4:11

In one sense, all who name the Name of Jesus will enter eternal rest with God. But, we may also know God's divine rest today.

We enter into God's rest by seeking His righteous order in our lives and living by to it. We enter by intently waiting upon God's specific guidance through the Word and prayer. We enter by knowing that God has already finished His work and prepared for our predicament. We enter by "setting our affections on things above, where Christ sits" (Col. 3:1)

We also enter into God's rest by physically rest-ing. This is what God specifically called the Israelites to do. By setting aside the seventh day, they acknowledged that they could not do it all and that they were dependent on God for all things. When you do not rest, could it be for you a lack of trust in God's sufficiency?

For a busy people . . .

Be encouraged.

Strength From the Word

"Thy word is a lamp unto my feet and a light unto my path" —Psalm 119:105

I have at times struggled with the issues of burnout and discouragement. What I have found is that these times occur mostly when I am not "prayed up" and consistently in God's word.

As a minister, I study God's Word to teach and prepare messages. Yet, I must also read and study for my own benefit. Neglecting times with God in prayer and meditation on the Word leaves us disconnected. It causes us to lack the affirmation and the inward guiding we need to walk by faith.

God calls us to meditate on His Word both day and night. (Ps. 1:2) Once you have spent time seeking the Lord in this way, several things will happen. I will only name a few.

1) You will be empowered. You will regain the correct sense that you are not standing alone. Your faith will be boosted and energized. (Rom. 10:17)
2) You will receive God's direction. Seeking God through His Word and prayer will give you both the right perspective and ground to stand on. You will be able to articulate why you are doing what you are doing with relation to the Word.

I encourage you take out time with God to address your concerns systematically and categorically. Search the Scriptures concerning these things and let the Holy Spirit speak to you as you read. It is my prayer that God's people will take God more seriously and will equip themselves to withstand the pressure of the world, "having done all to stand."

A Secure Salvation

> *He that believes on the Son of God has the*
> *testimony in himself . . . and this is the testi-*
> *mony: God has given us eternal life, and this*
> *life is in His Son. He who has the Son has*
> *life; he who does not have the Son of God*
> *does not have life. —1 John 5:10,11-12*

There can be no greater encouragement to our souls than the assurance that we will live eternally with God. It is such a joy time and again to watch a person's eyes light up as they come to know through faith in God's love that they will experience His eternal glory.

The Bible promises us we can know our eternal destiny. The Holy Spirit provides an inward witness. Writings in the New Testament reveal how this great confirmation by God's Spirit inflamed early Christians. Here are a few examples:

- Paul speaks of the witness of the Spirit that we are children of God. (Rom. 8:16; Gal. 4:6)
- He likens the Spirit's confirmation a "down-pay-ment" on our eternal reward. (2 Cor. 1:22)
- John quotes Jesus when he likens the witness of the Spirit to an overflowing spring. (John 4:14)

From this inward witness early Christians could pronounce, "these present sufferings are not even worthy to be compared to the glory that will be revealed in us." (Rom. 8:18)

Beloved, you can know God has a place for you. Believe the Word of God and this blessed assurance will be foundation for your Christian life.

God is Salvation

"Surely God is my salvation; I will trust and not be afraid. The Lord, the Lord, is my strength and my song; he has become my salvation." Isaiah 12:2

We are so blessed. It is wonderful to know God not only provides a way of salvation for us, but He has become our salvation. I read an illustration that will help you understand the difference between the two statements.

Once a man was traveling to the house of his friend and stopped for directions. The friend told him to go a certain distance in a certain direction and to make various turns here or there. After going through twisted roads and confusing pathways, the man found his way and made it to his friend's house, though very late.

On another occasion, the man started on the same trip. Yet, this time he had his friend in the car with him. The friend told him to turn right, turn left and even showed him some shortcuts. They made it to the house with time to spare.

It is so assuring to know that God not only shows on a map where we are to go, but becomes the "Living Map" as He guides us through His Holy Spirit.

May your heart be open to Him and be set to stand for Him today.

Confession

If we confess our sins, he is faithful and just and will forgive us our sins and purify us from all unrighteousness.– 1 John 1:9

God wants us to confess our sins. The word, "confess," means literally, "to agree with." The experience with God causes us acutely to recognize our sins. When this occurs, we are tempted to rationalize our sinfulness, calling our sins shortcomings, weaknesses, mistakes, indiscretions, and the like. These words do not make our actions any less wrong, but they do make us feel less like "bad people." The fact, however, is that we are sinners.

We are by nature "bad people." This may be hard to hear, but I have found it to be one of the most healing revelations. One must know one's sickness to be open to receive the grace to overcome it.

God does not reject us because of our nature. He should, but He does not. He would, but He has made provision for us. God knows we are "bad people" and He knows the bad thoughts, words and deeds with which we sin. Yet God does not condemn us and furthermore requires that we not condemn ourselves. He calls us to confess our sins and agree with Him that we are sinners in need of His grace. This realization of need will draw us closer to Him.

Know this and be encouraged.

Faithful Forgiveness

God, who has called you into fellowship with his Son Jesus Christ our Lord, is faithful. —1 Corinthians 1:9

I have at times experienced a break in fellowship with the God I love so much. The Bible teaches that we must maintain a pure heart to remain in fellowship with Him. Practically, this means that we must be continuously responsive to the Spirit of God. The Spirit leads us into all truth and reveals our sins so that we may mourn and confess them.

When we fall out of fellowship, we can feel lost and disheveled. Closeness to God grants a sense of God's love in wonderful ways. Sin disrupts our experience of this and makes God seem distant and far away. I encourage you, if you are in this state of mind, do not accept it! God is not far away. He is very near and, by His Spirit, He is dealing with you to deal with your sin.

The Word of God says that God loves you and is faithful. You must receive that by faith, even when your feelings suggest otherwise. It is easier to turn around and confess your faults when you know God is there waiting on you. Know that He is there and be encouraged.

Abide By the Voice

...and that you may love the Lord your God, listen to his voice, and hold fast to him. For the Lord is your life, and he will give you many years in the land he swore to give to your fathers, Abraham, Isaac and Jacob. —Deuteronomy 30:20

When seeking the Lord, I have at times missed God's answer because of contrary issues in my heart that I have ignored. Though God wants us to seek His face concerning all things, He will not often give fresh direction when we have ignored the prior prompting of His Spirit.

We must learn to relate to God on His terms. The issues that are so pressing to us are not to Him. God already has the answer. Thus, we must let God dictate the priorities regarding what gets dealt with first.

Do not ignore the promptings of the Holy Spirit when you think other issues are more important. Be sure to address His concerns before your own. In this way, you will create a great flow between you and God that will bring victory and sureness into you daily walk.

Be encouraged!

Rejoice!

Rejoice in the Lord and be glad, you righteous; sing, all you who are upright in heart! —Psalm 32:11

There is so much to rejoice about in the Lord. This Psalm reminds us of how blessed we truly are. It begins with the words, "Blessed is he whose transgression is forgiven and whose sin is covered." God accepts you and provides ways for you to experience His love in spite of your sinfulness. May you experienced the freedom that comes from knowing this.

The experience of God is wonderful. Sometimes there is a warm feeling. Sometimes there is a powerful presence within us. At times, the Spirit of God prompts us with courage, wisdom or some other kind of strength to do what we never thought we could. There is also the assurance of His direction. God speaks to us by the Holy Spirit through the Bible, prayer, our circumstances and the good counsel of other believers.

It is simply powerful to realize that God offers such a wonderful blessing in spite our not deserving it. This blessedness goes before us, follows us up, and causes us to walk with Him every step of the way. What a reason to rejoice!

Victory through Grace

No temptation has seized you except what is common to man. And God is faithful; he will not let you be tempted beyond what you can bear. But when you are tempted, he will also provide a way out so that you can stand up under it. —1 Corinthians 10:13

Grace is power. Some may think of grace as "God's permissive will" or "God looking over our faults and seeing our needs." There is a small measure of truth in these statements, but the Bible speaks of grace most often in a more powerful way.

Grace is God's favor. It is the power that He gives to enable us to do something. It is the power by which He "works all things together for good for those that love him and are called according to His purpose" (Rom. 8:28). In this passage we see grace in the ability to "escape temptation" and "stand up under it."

Please understand, when tempted to sin, sometimes we feel like we must deal with that sin by ourselves. In the worst of cases, we say, "I must keep myself from sinning lest God gets me." This is not how God wants us to handle it. God wants us to turn to His grace when we feel helplessly under stress. When we do, we will receive from Him the grace we need for the situation. (Heb. 4:16)

Be encouraged.

The Boundaries of Faith

Do not be anxious about anything, but in everything, by prayer and petition, with thanksgiving, present your requests to God. —Philippians 4:6

Faith can go only as far as prayer does. Exercising faith is not a mental game, where we just push negative thoughts out and hold on with great concentration to positive ones. Faith is simple. It is a direct response to God as He makes His will known through His Holy Spirit and His Word.

Prayer is communication with God. It is the part of our Christian life that makes things work. It connects the dots. On one hand, we have God's will and power and on the other we have the promises of His revealed Word. Thirdly, we have ourselves—our will and our faith. These three areas are well separated from each other and must be bridged. Prayer bridges this gap.

When we pray, we enter into an experience with God. The Holy Spirit shows up to reveal God's will and opens the Scriptures to our understanding. He enlivens the words on the Biblical page and speaks directly to our situations. Through this experience we can respond directly to God.

Without prayer we are left with shots in the dark, at one moment believing we are doing God's will and at another doubting. Prayer settles this. We know, in spite of whatever happens, we are rightfully discerning God's Word and it will come to pass. This is how we can be anxious for nothing. Our faith must be activated by prayer.

Be encouraged.

The Fear of the Lord

Therefore, my dear friends, as you have always obeyed– not only in my presence, but now much more in my absence– continue to work out your salvation with fear and trembling, for it is God who works in you to will and to act according to his good purpose. —Philippians 2:12-13

The fear of the Lord is essential to our relationship with Him. The Bible teaches that the fear of the Lord is the hatred of evil. The early church was healthy and grew tremendously because they feared God. (Acts 9:31) It is through the fear of the Lord that we experience God's glory.

The fear of God is probably one of the most misunderstood principles in the Word. Sometimes we confuse it with "being afraid of God." This is not quite the point. The fear of the Lord is the recognition of God's awesomeness, power and righteousness judgment (wrath) in our lives and in the earth. It is the careful demeanor we take on when we approach someone nobler and greater than ourselves. It is the respect for righteous authority, where we know that transgression means punishment, but we are thankful because the requirements are for our own good.

The holy and awesome God of the Universe is taking precious time to work in our lives. With great care and planning He is working to change us from the inside out so that we will both "will and do his good pleasure." We must recognize God's hand in our lives with an appropriate "fear and trembling" and be careful not to resist it or work against it. It is a precious thing for the holy God to take interest and to work in our lives.

Be encouraged.

The Power of Godliness

. . . having a form of godliness but denying its power. Have nothing to do with them.
— *2 Timothy 3:5*

Beloved, we must make a decision. Will we live for God, or will we not? Will we set our hearts on things above, or will we make our beds with those below? We must decide whether we will truly live a blessed godly life, or perpetrate as though we did.

There is a power that comes with godliness. It is the power of transformation and the power of love. This power is important because by it, we witness to the truth of the Cross and the life-changing love of God. We must witness not only to the existence of God, but to His power in our lives. It is a tremendous blessing, but also a requirement that we experience God. Consider the words of Paul:

"My message and my preaching were not with wise and persuasive words, but with a demonstration of the Spirit's power, so that your faith might not rest on men's wisdom, but on God's power" (1 Cor. 2:4-5).

Meditate on this and be encouraged.

Spiritual Life

Do not get drunk on wine, which leads to debauchery. Instead, be filled with the Spirit. —Ephesians 5:18

The Spirit-filled life is so very different from the religious life. In the religious life, we "catch the spirit." In the Spirit-filled life, the Spirit leads us. In the religious life, we look for a good time. The Spirit-filled person looks for purpose. Religious people try to be good people. Spiritual people realize the extent of their sinfulness and pray for mercy.

Religious folk are concerned about their earthly church; Spirit-filled people are concerned about being the church on earth for the heavenly kingdom. Religious people consider how far they can go and still be in the will of God. Spirit-filled people are enraptured by the experience of God and dare not even think of disrupting that blessed fellowship. Religious people look for an experience from God; Spirit-filled people know and experience the fulness of God Himself.

Being Spirit-filled is something "better felt than told." It seems subtle, but there is a world of difference between the two.

May you know the awesome power of the Spirit-filled life.

Be Ready to Listen

Turn at my rebuke; Surely I will pour out my Spirit on you; I will make my words known to you. —Proverbs. 1:23

The wisdom of the Lord is not hard to find. Actually, the Bible teaches God's wisdom is readily available, and even actively seeks us out. "Wisdom calls aloud outside; she raises her voice in the open squares" (v. 20).

I have found that commonly, before I even ask God for direction or guidance, He has placed the answer before me. It has long been said, "while we are trying to figure it out, God has already worked it out." This is a powerful truth. God is not waiting for us to explain our situation to Him for Him to try to figure things out. Before we even know our need, God as our Heavenly Parent has made provisions.

The object of being led, then, is being sensitive and aware of the Spirit's promptings throughout our day. In the verse above, the Word says, "turn at my rebuke." In other words, "listen up, I've got a better thing for you—I've got a better way to go." The Spirit of God is actively working to get our attention and we can hear Him if we listen.

The Spirit Speaks

The Spirit himself testifies with our spirit that we are God's children. —Romans 8:16

Some may wonder why the Spirit does not speak more audibly. Actually, sometimes He does. But, a story from my past may illuminate why He usually speaks in a "still small voice."

When my father was alive, I believed he was the wisest man I knew. Everybody seemed to come to him for advice. However, there were times his advice, though correct, was hard to take. People would begin arguing with him and sometimes even become irrate. My father on the other hand would remain calm and always speak in a quiet tone. In fact, the louder a person got, the quieter my father got. Once, a man said to my dad, "why do not you just speak up; I cannot hear you!" My father replied, "If you wanted to hear me, you would listen."

God wants us to listen. "Those that have ears to hear, let them hear what the Spirit says."

Sufficient Grace

But He said to me, "My grace is sufficient for you, for my power is made perfect in weakness." —2 Corinthians 12:9

What do you do when God does not answer your prayers? How do we deal with our Father's apparent silence at certain tragedy in our lives? Surely God cares for you. What seems like His silence is actually Him drawing you closer.

Paul prayed because of some infirmity or major problem that clearly vexed his spirit. When he brought it to the Father, there was no reply. Paul, however, did not lose confidence in the One whom he had placed all his hope. He prayed again. Still . . . no answer. It would seem that God should be more available this, one of his choice servants. Paul did not take "no" answer for an answer. He besought the Lord again.

On this third time, there was no miracle. There was no mighty vision. Paul did not receive the overwhelming experience comparable to that of his conversion. Instead, a still voice whispered to him, "My grace is sufficient for you."

Beloved, God will always answer your prayers. Silence is not an answer. When silence follows your request, this is an indication to persist and to draw closer to God. Never give up on prayer. Be encouraged.

Getting Prayers Answered

If you remain in me and my words remain in you, ask whatever you wish, and it will be given you. —John 15:7

Often when seeking answered prayer, we ask ourselves whether or not the request is according to God's will. I believe the real question is, however, are we living according to God's will. The assurance of answered prayer begins not with the condition of the request, but the condition of our hearts.

The Word of Christ teaches us that answered prayer is the property of those who follow after the Spirit and live according to God's Word. In other words, when our minds are set on the Spirit's prompting, our hearts are set on things above, and our minds set to learn from God's Word His will, His ways and His purpose, we have prepared ourselves for the wonderful experience of consistently answered prayer.

Never settle for unanswered prayer. God always answers and we will know His answers when the proper conditions are met.

Be encouraged.

Good Works

There remains, then, a Sabbath-rest for the people of God; for anyone who enters God's rest also rests from his own work, just as God did from His. —Hebrews 4:9

I once had a shocking realization after working a job for over a year. I worked hard, but I found myself exhausted and never able to complete all my tasks. The harder I worked, the worse it seemed. As I prayed about this God showed me what was going on. The revelation was this: I spent about 80% of my time working at working and only 20% actually fulfilling the purpose.

I would like to share with you a few symptoms of my condition: 1) small victories, if any, following massive amounts of effort; 2) great planning with horrible follow-through; 3) no quality time for prayer; and 4) great determination ending in terrible frustration.

At first, I worked harder at communication and scheduling. I got up earlier in the day and stayed up later at night. I worked creatively to coordinate the efforts of my team and build team spirit and cooperation. I even set aside more time in my schedule for praying for success. It was not until this revelation that I realized all of my efforts were what the Bible calls "dead works."

"Dead works" are what we do in our own strength

for our own purposes. We are to turn from dead works to following Christ. God is always at work around us and invites us to join in that work. In our secular jobs, our families, our friendships, etc., God has an assignment for us and will bless our work if we put Him first.

The Blessing of Contentment

But godliness with contentment is great gain. —1 Timothy 6:6

Contentment is one of the greatest assets of the Christian walk. Often things will not be easy in our lives. We will have "ups and downs." Jesus warns us in the Word that tribulation is a part of life. (John 16:33) Yet, when we possess the virtue of contentment, we can be blessed in spite of our circumstances.

Contentment is learned. (Phil. 4:11-13) It does not come naturally simply because we are Christian. It comes with growth.

Contentment comes when we learn to trust God in the difficult seasons. We cannot just discover some principles about contentment and put them into practice. Once we are saved, our lives go through the process of sanctification; in other words, by the work of the Holy Spirit, we are made more like Christ.

This process often takes us through difficult experiences. Sometimes we may even feel like we cannot take it another day! We must trust the Lord. We must make up in our minds if we believe two things: 1) God is able, and 2) God loves us unconditionally. When we consistently trust God and hold firmly to our knowledge of His love and power, we will learn contentment.

I encourage you today to know the love of Christ and be filled with the fulness of God. (Eph. 3:20)

The Cross

But whatever was to my profit I now consider loss for the sake of Christ.
—Philippians 3:7

Once I dreamed of the Cross of Christ. It was off in the distance, but I so much wanted it to be near. In the distance, I could forget it. It was real to me, but had no forceful claim on my life. After seeing it afar off, it happened in the dream that the cross was brought near me. I heard a question asked, "Since he has died for you, can you not at least get up for him." Then, I woke up.

The cross is the key to powerful and passionate Christian living. But, we must know it intimately, not casually. We must know it close up. An old wise saying goes like this: "You do not know a man until you have walked a day in his moccasins." This is the kind of knowledge to which Paul referred when he said: "What is more, I consider everything a loss compared to the surpassing greatness of knowing Christ Jesus my Lord, for whose sake I have lost all things." (Phil. 3:8)

Do you want to really know him? Do you want to be bathed in his love? Impress your mind with the death, burial and resurrection of Jesus. Learn to recklessly abandon your wants and desires and seek to see Christ wholeheartedly.

Those who have ears to hear, let them hear what the Spirit is saying to the Church.

The Glory in Us

For the earth will be filled with the knowledge of the glory of the Lord, as the waters cover the sea. —Habakkuk 2:14

In a soon coming day, everyone will be filled with the knowledge of the glory of the LORD. No one will have to say, "Teach me of the Lord," because everyone will know Him personally. But until that day, God has chosen to show forth His glory in and through we who believe.

Our lives are to be examples of the beauty and majesty of the Lord. We obviously cannot do this in and of ourselves. But, the longer we stay close to His glorious presence in the spirit of worship, the more our lives will glow with His light.

How does the Bible prescribe that we do this? It says, "Therefore, I urge you, brothers, in view of God's mercy, to offer your bodies as living sacrifices, holy and pleasing to God—this is your spiritual act of worship" (Rom. 12:1) Worship is not just done on Sunday. We must intentionally give ourselves to God daily for His pleasure and use.

Passion for Witnessing

I will declare your name to my brothers; in the congregation I will praise you.
—Psalm 22:22

We should have an excitement about talking about God to others. Our experience of God should be such that we cannot hold in our joy. I have learned that we can have such a joy in our hearts on a consistent basis. We fuel it when we share it with others.

The Church learned centuries ago the importance of confessing faith with and to others. In many churches there is a part of the service where the entire congregation recites a confession of faith. This was started to add vibrancy and excitement to the walk of faith, but it has become rote and often dry. I believe this is so because we do it without any personal reflection.

We should learn to think often of what God has done for us and how we have experienced His divine hand in our lives. We should often share our stories with others. As we bear witness of what God has done, we enliven our faith and place ourselves in position to be powerfully used of God in someone else's life.

Share something of your faith today and be encouraged.

A Passion for Christ

Speak to one another with psalms, hymns and spiritual songs. Sing and make music in your heart to the Lord. —Ephesians 5:19

It has been said that music is medicine for the soul. This is a powerful observation. Music affects our moods. It can soothe or generate anxiety. It is a communication that bypasses our intellect and speaks straight to our heart—sometimes down to the very core.

Think of a motion picture without music and incidental sounds. What about an evening out on the town without music? It is impossible to imagine.

Melodies come from the heart and go to the heart. We encourage ourselves and other believers in a spirit of worship when we share in spiritual songs. Do you want a rich and fulfilling love relationship with God? Try "making music in your heart to God."

Think about a love relationship like marriage. For many marriages, things start with a bang and lull to a complacent hum. The relationship becomes common and the romance diminishes. Things are no different with our relationship with God. We have to learn to keep the excitement going. If we are to worship the Lord in the beauty of holiness, let us use more than words or dutiful actions. Let us sing unto the Lord the songs of our heart.

Purity

Since we have these promises, dear friends, let us purify ourselves from everything that contaminates body and spirit, perfecting holiness out of reverence for God. —2 Corinthians 7:1

It is through the purity of heart that we see God. This is a first act of faith. As we live by faith, we must learn to have faith for a clean heart. Without this purity, we miss so much of God and His blessings.

We purify our hearts by singlemindedly seeking God in faith. We decide in every situation that we want God more than anything else. This can be difficult to keep up, but when we seek God's help through prayer, He divinely aids us through His Spirit.

Keeping a pure heart is our responsibility, but it is done by God's grace and power. We must learn to exercise our faith in this matter and trust God to help us as we seek Him.

Be encouraged.

A Quality of Faith

Blessed is the one who reads the words of this prophecy, and blessed are those who hear it and take to heart what is written in it, because the time is near. —Revelation 1:3

How does one prevent the pressures of life from choking out their seriousness about the Lord? For many of us, as soon as we find a good "rhythm" in our Christian walk and start growing, many things arise to set us off the path. How do we remain consistent in our walk with Christ? The answer lies in the quality of our faith.

Three things have helped strengthen my faith: perspective, prayer and persistence. If we will be consistent in Christ, we must maintain a "faith perspective." We must learn through God's Word to see things as He does. Though He will not show us the big picture, He will give us enough by which to go. (Deut. 29:29)

Start praying in every situation. Pray in tongues if you are gifted that way. Let your mind keep coming back to prayer. Feed your prayer life with daily meditations. When you get into the Bible morning and evening, this will give you direction and things for which you can pray. You will see answers and these will strengthen and encourage your faith.

As for persistence, whatever you do, "never, never, never give up!" Kill self-condemnation and claim God's grace. Find the promises of God's grace and forgiveness in the Bible and confess them aloud. Because you are God's child, you cannot lose! Be persistent. Know the urgency of the time, beloved, and let us get serious about our walk with Christ.

Be encouraged.

Enlightening Paths

Direct me in the path of your commands,
for there I find delight. —Psalm 119:35

It is hard to hear the guiding voice of the Spirit when our habit is not to walk according to written Word of God.

God's Word gives direction and principles. It directs us in seeking His kingdom and causing His praise to fill the earth. His principles teach us how to behave and live with virtue and integrity. When we live by these things, the inward voice of the Lord becomes clear to us. Outside them, we will hear nothing but confusion. I encourage you: discipline your life and build godly character.

How do you hear from the Lord? How do you know it is Him and not another? You know by knowing His heart and by imitating His character. Stay in your Bible and pray always. Make hearing from God daily of utmost importance. His voice is clear and discernable when we are submitted to the way of His Word. Yet, should our lives center on selfishness and friendship with the world, even the best of us can lose our hearing.

Be encouraged.

Knowing Him

That I may know him, and the power of his resurrection, and the fellowship of his sufferings, being made conformable unto his death. —Philippians 3:10 (KJV)

How badly do you want to know Jesus? Many people "know" the Lord, but only on a surface level. This is to say, they know about him and have him as a mere acquaintance. I have seen fewer people who have been enraptured by an intimate knowledge of him.

An intimate knowledge of Christ brings us in touch with God's nature. It is something to be greatly desired. When we truly encounter God's nature—that is, who God really is—we are brought into awe and a holy fear. Something within our hearts should stand at attention in His presence. It is not something we must think about, it simply happens. The light of God's glory is penetrating and His very Name is power. Ultimate power brings respect, as well as safety and comfort.

We cannot know the riches of God's glory except that we die to ourselves. Let us be clear on this one thing: dying to self is not the goal, but it is necessary for us truly to see his face. Do not strive to die, strive to see Him and dying will automatically present itself. When it does, the appropriate response is to submit to it. It will look ugly and often present a very real and ugly crisis. The question is: Is God really worth it to you?

Will you know Jesus as he wants to be known?

Faith for Doubting Hearts

"I tell you the truth, if anyone says to this mountain, 'Go, throw yourself into the sea,' and does not doubt in his heart but believes that what he says will happen, it will be done for him. —Mark 11:23

Great things happen for those who believe God without doubting. However, it is sometimes very difficult to surmount the doubt that is in our hearts. This is because we try to fight our doubting with our willpower or reasoning, and not spiritually.

Doubt is a hesitation or second-guessing that is an affront to God. It comes mainly from a heart callused by sin and willfulness. The Bible calls this "hardheartedness." Every sin we commit in willfulness hardens our heart. Every "no" to God and every "yes" to flesh adds more to our callousness.

The Bible has absolutely no toleration for a rejection of God's commands. This may sound hard, but it is not. On our jobs, we learn the culture of the office. In the armed service, soldiers learn a certain way of life. There is mercy, but there is a standard for which we are accountable. We must learn again how to walk with God respecting the nature of who He is.

As we commit to this, God can soften our hearts. God wants so much to show us the riches of His glory. He is so very remorseful that so many of His children forgo walking closely with Him because of their laziness, lack of respect and complacency. Let us learn His way and walk in it. He loves us and is waiting.

Authority and the World

"By what authority are you doing these things?" they asked. "And who gave you this authority?" —Matthew 21:23

It can be difficult sharing your faith in hostile environments. We are told not to mention the name of Jesus at school, on the job, in public meetings, etc.. How do we deal with this pressure and provide an uncompromising witness of Jesus Christ in the world?

Do all you can to live out the Word of God with integrity and commitment. Avoid contradicting your witness with what you say or do. Apply God's wisdom to your life and live victoriously. Do not try to be perfect, do your best to live unto God. Your personal character is the foundation of your witnessing authority.

When you witness at work, let God open doors for you. You are anointed. You have a light. Let it shine. You do not need to be boisterous or forceful with people. Just be the "you" God wants you to be and He will draw people to you. When they come, do not be ashamed of who you are. Let them know where you stand up front. Do not try to "sneak God in."

Authority in the Christian's life involves acting with wisdom. The Bible says, "The fruit of the righteous is a tree of life, and he who wins souls is wise" (Prov. 11:30).

Meditate on this and be encouraged.

Asking Properly

. . . since you have not asked for a long life but for wisdom and knowledge to govern my people over whom I have made you king, therefore wisdom and knowledge will be given you. And I will also give you wealth, riches and honor . . . —2 Chronicles 1:11-12

Know what is proper in prayer. We should not ask for things which transfers control from God's hands to our own. God wants that when we ask things of Him, we become more dependant on Him and less on ourselves.

Provision from God should not be seen as an elusive, difficult boon. It is His good pleasure to provide for us and to care for our needs and desires. Yet, we must go to Him with faith, ever trusting Him to see about even our smallest needs.

Consider what you ask of God. He takes no pleasure in providing us means to live without Him. Is what you ask for personal desire, a sense of security or for esteem? Beloved, He wants you to find these things in Him. When you are set firmly in Him, you will be ready to handle the blessings He wants to shower on you.

Seek Him in faith and be encouraged.

Defeat Worry

Some seed fell among thorns, which grew up and choked the plants . . . . The one who received the seed that fell among the thorns is the man who hears the word, but the worries of this life and the deceitfulness of wealth choke it, making it unfruitful. —Matthew 13:7,22

Do not let the Word of life be choked out of you! Surely, it will cause you to leave conversations by the water-hole at your job and make you chagrin when course jokes are being told. It will cause you to be ridiculed for not compromising what is right. You will be persecuted because you know better and you are committed to do better.

Beloved, please know these worries of life come only to make you unfruitful in Christ. However, there are souls that are waiting for real Christians to stand up. People will only see the truth if we are willing to stand against all opposition and deceitfulness for the truth. People need to see our fire, our excitement, our blessedness.

These things can only be exemplified if we "just do not care" what happens. Take your mind off your concerns and rest in Christ. Never let anything choke the Life of God out of you!

God's Refreshing

I will refresh the weary and satisfy the faint. —Jeremiah 31:25

Know that as you press toward your purpose in life—or to be more precise, "press on in your purpose"—God will sustain you. Though you may not know from which way He will come, the Lord of mercy will find you when you really need him.

The refreshing of God is an amazing experience. We are told: "hope does not disappoint us, because God has poured out his love into our hearts by the Holy Spirit, whom he has given us" (Rom. 5:5). This is a supernatural experience. I tell you the truth, in the times when you have truly spent your last portion of strength you will find strength to stand in Him.

The refreshing of the Lord is something better felt than told. It comes automatically because of His love, though we must receive it by faith. Thus, surrender your circumstances to Him and look for your blessing! God will see you though, beloved. He loves you and will refresh you.

Be encouraged.

Staying on Point

*Whenever the cloud lifted from above the
Tent, the Israelites set out; wherever the
cloud settled, the Israelites encamped.
—Numbers 9:17*

How often has the Lord given you direction and
you were slack or negligent to obey it? How often
does the Lord have to tell us to do something? We
must learn to keep the charge of the Lord, keeping
His guiding Word at the forefront of our thoughts.

I have learned this through experience. In one
case, I sought the Lord for healing of a minor affliction. The Lord directed me in a way through which
He would do it. Yet, though I consider the Word as
paramount in my life, my actions did not show this.
I did not take the guidance of the Lord seriously
enough. I realized now that God wanted to do more
than heal me. Through the healing, He wanted to
build my faith and responsiveness to His proceeding
Word.

It is important to learn how to follow the Lord.
This is a skill we must learn. Like a child, we must be
trained to hear and respond to God's voice. God will
teach us through "gentle" correction and instruction.
Be open to this process and learn obedience.

Be encouraged.

Quickly Come

He who testifies to these things says, "Yes, I am coming soon." Amen. Come, Lord Jesus. —Revelation 22:20

"Come, Lord Jesus!" Is this the cry of your heart? Of all that we do in worship and service, this sentiment must be at the forefront. The coming of Christ is our great hope, though I find few that talk of this and seem to yearn for it.

Many say, "the presence of the Lord, the presence of the Lord," and make broad and grand statements about the glory of God during worship experiences. I declare to you that we will feel his presence no more profoundly than when Christ returns in bodily form. It will be more than glorious.

The yearning for the Lord's coming is not shallow and cavalier. It cements the right motivations in us. When our hearts cry out for his coming, it puts everything else in perspective and helps us rank what is really important in our Christian lives.

"Come, Lord Jesus!" must be the cry of the Church again. It is the center of our mission and the spirit of prophecy. Let us seek after his coming with great expectation and great preparation. Jesus' second coming is the fact for which all of history is calling. No one can rightly deny it will be fulfilled and this means everybody will be accountable.

Yes! Come Lord Jesus, quickly come.

Overcoming Criticism

In your anger do not sin; when you are on your beds, search your hearts and be silent. Selah —Psalm 4:4

Criticism is one of the greatest disrupters of a peaceful spirit. I venture to say that most people have a hard time with it. We all have been set at edge my a critical remark or a judgmental stare. Yet, criticism can be a great ally.

We must know how to receive criticism. I sometimes become angry when criticized. Yet, the Scripture teaches that "in our anger, do not sin." We should learn to listen to the opinions of others, even when they are crass or thoughtless in their expression of them.

Let us learn to find a quiet place and to "search our heart." We must know our own mind. Sometimes we must face some opposition to prove our position is solid. We must account for the possibility that we are wrong. Whatever the verdict, we find ourselves stronger and wiser when we take time in solitude to consider our ways.

Opposition will always come; it is how we handle it that counts. May this be a blessing to you.

Don't Lead from Behind

Listen, my son, and be wise, and keep your heart on the right path. —Proverbs 23:19

It is easy to react rather than to act. Arguments rise from reacting. Divorces begin here. Wars arise from one comparatively small offense. What can be said about reacting? It is deadly.

God has instructed us concerning this trap. He says in His Word, "But I tell you: Love your enemies and pray for those who persecute you" (Matt. 5:44) and again, "Bless those who persecute you; bless and do not curse" (Rom. 12:14). These were not admonitions to allow someone to take advantage of you. These were power principles for you to bring God's order to bear.

God wants us, as Christians, to be leaders in all things. Leaders do not blindly and impulsively react. When someone finds bad in us, we must find good in them and make them to know it! When someone offends us, we must bless them and show them our truest leaning. There is sin enough in each of our lives for the whole world to be offended. Yet, God's grace has covered us and is purposed to work through us to help cover others. "Love covers a multitude of sins," saith the Lord. (1 Pet. 4:8)

Be encouraged.

God Remembers

But God remembered Noah . . . —Genesis 8:1

God judged the earth in a mighty act, causing waters to overflow the mountains. No less remarkable is how God caused the waters to recede afterward. Yet, the most amazing fact to note is why God receded the water. The Bible says, "But God remembered Noah. . . ."

There is nothing worse in a Christian's life than to feel forgotten by God. We all experience this feeling once and again. When chaotic waters overflow our lives and our feet are far from being firmly planted on the ground, the feeling of abandonment bombards even the strongest of us. Even faith-filled Noah was reluctant to get out of the boat after the flood.

Take hope that God always remembers. Let your faith be strengthened through knowing God never changes. Out of His love for one man, God changed the face of the entire earth and He loves you just the same. Is it not amazing?

Managing Authority

"By what authority are you doing these things?" they asked. "And who gave you this authority?" —Matthew 21:23

Intimidation, the "fear factor," is a fiery dart often used by the Enemy to destroy our Christian witness and abundant life. It has been said, "If you do not take and use the authority vested in you, someone else will take it and use it against you." I have found this to be true.

Authority is not only for people in leadership positions. Everybody has vested authority, and, to note, being in Christ is about learning to walk in that God-given authority. I say again: the Christian life is the process of walking in your God-given authority.

The key to walking in your authority is knowing who God says you are and being that person. This requires boldness and can be very uncomfortable because, as God's child, you do not fit in the world. You will offend. But, more importantly, many will see the light through your witness.

Be all that God has called you to be and be encouraged.

Flow in Favor

Therefore, since through God's mercy we have this ministry, we do not lose heart.
—2 Corinthians 4:1

It is amazing to watch God day after day open doors we by ourselves could not even see. It is wonderful to be able to point to specific, clear moments when He intervened and saved the day. There is nothing greater than to reflect on His manifested love in our lives—not only "how He loves us," but "when He loves us." It is exciting to kneel down in prayer and know that God will answer.

This is incentive for living the Christian life. Turning from the pleasures of sin is hard unless there is some incentive. Forsaking the ties to this world is quite nearly impossible except we have the foretaste of eternal rewards. God gives us an earnest of the glories to come. He gives us a taste. When we experience His favor, we are inwardly strengthened to go all the way with Jesus.

We must learn to flow in the favor of God and remain encouraged in our Christian walk. We must learn to trust Him, to wait on Him and to want only Him. When we do this, we will never again read about the abundant life Jesus promised and wonder what it is.

Be encouraged.

Helpfulness

For I know your eagerness to help . . .
—2 Corinthians 9:2

One of the greatest aspects of the Christian life is the drive to help others. This is a potent way of living out the life of Christ. I believe a Christian's personal witness is aided in no greater way than to have a lifestyle of helping others.

Many of us have a heart to help someone in need randomly. This heart is very important to have. However, what about being committed to helping someone regularly? This may be taking an elderly or disabled neighbor to the grocery store or taking small gifts to random patients in a hospital. You can visit strangers in a nursing home or stand outside watching over the children who play on your block.

All of us have something we can give and something we can do to share God's love with our neighbor. When you get directly involved in someone's life, you will never regret it. What can you do?

Be encouraged.

Simply Christian

The disciples were called Christians first at Antioch. —Acts 11:26

There are so many things that disrupt our simplicity. These weights and distractions for all of us at one time or another make being a Christian seem complex and difficult. Yet, it ought not be this way regularly.

How can we live "simply Christian" in these days and times? I am learning that it requires character and a sincere commitment to principle. By this, I mean that we must take charge of our lives and know for what we will or will not stand. So much of our lives fall in disarray because we are either ignorant of the principles of God's Word or too fearful to stand by them.

You can take charge of your life. God is in control and will "work all things together" to enable you to walk in freedom. It usually takes time and you will face moments when you feel like you are not getting anywhere. Commit to the process anyway. God is in control and wants you to take charge.

Be encouraged.

Why Go to Bible Study?

All Scripture is God-breathed and is useful for teaching, rebuking, correcting and training in righteousness, so that the man of God may be thoroughly equipped for every good work. —2 Timothy 3:16-17

Why should we go to Bible Study? Public study of the Word such as midweek classes, small groups, and Sunday School classes are wonderful in teaching the content and principles of God's Word. They can excite, inspire, comfort, inform and even motivate us. But ultimately, they must equip us for the good works God has for us.

The greatest problem in many Bible Studies is that students are not able to apply what they are being taught to their ministries and areas of service. If your Bible Study is truly to be effective, it not only requires a good teacher and study, it requires a genuine seeking on the learner's part.

Be encouraged to search out the good works God has for you and learn principles from God's Word to sustain them.

Abundance

Now to him who is able to do immeasurably more than all we ask or imagine, according to his power that is at work within us . . . —Ephesians 3:20

God's trademark is abundance. When He blesses us, our cups run over. When we give, He gives back to us in a way that is "pressed down, shaken together and running over." Abundance is God's signature that testifies to others of His wonderful grace and power available to those He loves.

God wants us to walk in abundance so that we may share His goodness with others. (2 Cor. 9:10) We should not spend our blessings on selfish desires (Jas. 4:3). Rather, let us praise Him for them and reveal to others the depths of His love. (Eph. 3:16-18)

There are three steps to walking in abundance. The blessing is available to everyone, but we must follow these steps to experience it. We must prioritize God's plan and agenda for our lives, we must be diligent in what we do, and we must consistently share our blessings with others. When these three steps are applied, we will be constantly amazed at how God moves in our lives.

Be encouraged.

Counting on God

And my God will meet all your needs according to his glorious riches in Christ Jesus. —Philippians 4:19

It is one thing to believe God meets your needs. It is another to count on this. It is one thing to know God is good; it is another to depend on His goodness. God wants us to live our lives where we become dependant on nothing and no one else but Him. He wants us to count on Him for our every need.

God is gentle with us. He knows we must learn to count on Him. This learning takes time. Thus, He gives us challenges that we can surely handle. These tests may seem like crises, but as we get through them we realize how small they really are.

The key to counting on God is taking each step as it comes. Do not be afraid or back down. Learn from each affair—both when you do well and when you do not. Build your faith, beloved, and be encouraged.

Hold on to Jesus

You will keep in perfect peace him whose mind is steadfast, because he trusts in you.
—Isaiah 26:3

There are times in our lives when we need almost forcibly to hold on to peace. Peace is the highest commodity when tragedy and devastating circumstances arise. In the face of loss, divorce, personal trauma or death, a sense of inner peace makes all the difference.

What do you do when your peace is gone? Where can you go to find answers to help a friend facing hard times? I have learned by experience that Jesus really is the answer.

The Bible says, ". . . the mind controlled by the Spirit is life and peace" (Rom. 8:6). When we are in Christ, He provides the Holy Spirit to aid us and give us strength. When we are stretched beyond our limits, we are not stretched beyond His. He gives a strength to our spirits we never knew we had available to us. We simply have to call on Him in faith.

You can deny it if you please, however as a Christian you know inwardly that this precious power is available to you. Claim it, my friends, and be encouraged.

The Power of Inspiration

Jesus answered her, "If you knew the gift of God and who it is that asks you for a drink, you would have asked him and he would have given you living water."
—John 4:10

A powerful part of our Lord Jesus' ministry was his innate ability to take what was in him and share it with others. Jesus inspired people. Yes, he was bold and brilliant. He was charismatic and compassionate. But, the added dimension for Christ was his power to open himself up to people and to share with them heart to heart.

To inspire like Jesus did, we must first be convinced of how blessed we truly are. We come to know this as we are filled with the Spirit. When we live our lives full of faith, our cup of blessings runs over. It is of this overflow that we bless and inspire others.

Beware of the danger of being myopic and blind in reflecting on how God has blessed you. It is truly wonderful to get what we need for our flesh, but the richest blessings are spiritual. Search out His promises and rejoice over the victory in your life that they bring. Then, you will be all the more inspiring.

Be encouraged.

The Holy Spirit

"Do not leave Jerusalem, but wait for the gift my Father promised, which you have heard me speak about." —Acts 1:4

We are so honored and blessed to have the Holy Spirit reside within us. What a glorious and mind-boggling privilege! By Him, Christ lives in us and we may boast of abiding in the Lord. By Him, we are made new and daily set on the right path. By Him, our Father draws near as we draw close to Him. How can we discount so great a blessing?

The Holy Spirit indwells us, renewing and restoring our lives to the image and pattern for which they were created. As the Promised One, He gives us hearts of flesh for our hearts of stone. (Ezek. 11:19) He also fills us, giving us power to live out Christ's life. Greater measures of the Spirit are ours for the asking. (Luke 11:13) God's Spirit drives us to maturity, where we can be "filled with the fullness of God." He powerfully speaks into our spirits that we are God's children. (Rom. 8:14)

The Holy Spirit works in us and around us. He is in us, but we can also be in Him. As we are in the Spirit, we praise and worship the true and living God. He draws near to us in His manifest presence. The Spirit makes this possible, for only in the Spirit can we encounter God and not die.

Praise God for His wonderful promise and gift.

What joy we have at the thought of His presence with and in us.

A Full Plate

Very early in the morning, while it was still dark, Jesus got up, left the house and went off to a solitary place, where he prayed.
—Mark 1:35

Everybody is busy and getting busier. When do we get time for devotional prayer, writing in our personal journals, spending time with family, church, exercising or resting? It seems no matter what we do, there is more to do. We all have a full plate and it is exhausting.

There is so much pressing on us, yet this was not unlike the life Jesus led while on the earth. He was pressed so much that there came a point he could not even enter a city for a comfortable stay. How did Jesus handle it? He prayed.

Jesus rose very early to pray and seek God. What He knew about the Father caused him to sacrifice time for some much needed sleep to be in prayer. His prayer time enabled him to deal with the pressures he faced daily.

I encourage you today to seek to know God in this kind of way. How do you do it? You ask Him and let His Spirit lead you. You may have asked Him before, but did you let Him lead you? When the Spirit leads, it will certainly change your perspective on life. Be prepared for this. But, the end will be more wonderful than the beginning.

Be encouraged.

Excellence and Humility

You may say to yourself, "My power and the strength of my hands have produced this wealth for me." —Deuteronomy 8:17

The greatest enemy of excellence is pride. The second greatest is envy. These two vices are subtle and work by slowly eroding away at our character. Yet, when we set our minds to the standard of excellence, we become very vulnerable to their encroachments.

When we walk in a spirit of excellence, we must also firmly hold to the spirit of humility. Let us remember that we seek excellence not for the attainment of status or stuff. We must not seek it so that we can "look good." This is using outward things to believe in ourselves. By this, we build our confidence on things that will not last.

Build your confidence on God's unchanging love for you and His unmerited grace. Seek excellence being motivated by mercy, not pride or envy. Beware of the encroachments of the latter two. When you see them, humble yourself quickly and confess your sin. God does not want you to settle for less and this is based on His honor, not yours.

Be encouraged.

Lead Yourself

If it is leadership, let him govern diligently. —Romans 12:8

Never surrender your leadership of yourself. True leadership begins with the diligent governing of one's character. This kind of leadership is powerful and effective.

Those with this understanding, know the power of a "made-up mind." They base their commitments on facts, not feelings. They throw their whole heart behind their decisions, but do not "follow their hearts" in making decisions. Leaders are courageous and "gutsy," but operate on wisdom and principle. Leadership takes character.

It is powerful when we become leaders over ourselves. The Bible says, "Better a patient man than a warrior, a man who controls his temper than one who takes a city" (Prov. 16:32). On the other hand, it says, "Like a city whose walls are broken down is a man who lacks self-control" (Prov. 25:28). When we lead through character, we can take cities. But, without character, we are consistently shaken and controlled by others and our circumstances.

God made all of us to be leaders. When we lead ourselves, we garner the power of influence that then enables us to help others become the leaders they were meant to be. Be a leader, beloved, and be encouraged.

What Makes a Leader

When the angel of the Lord appeared to Gideon, he said, "The Lord is with you, mighty warrior." —Judges 6:12

God has made us all to be leaders, though we may not know it. He has appointed each of us a responsibility to lead and to make a difference. The task may be pubic or in private; it may be in a position of leadership, or as humble helper. Whatever the case, God wants you to lead and calls you "mighty."

Leadership comes ultimately from God's appointment. When God gives you a task and you set yourself to do it diligently, you are a leader. You may or may not have the gifts you think are significant; your circumstance may be grim. But, God has appointed you for such a time as this. Take notice, "the Lord is with you!"

I remember being very shy as a child. During one school play, I so wanted to play a part, but "I couldn't sing, I couldn't dance, and I wasn't good enough with remembering my lines." I was not a leader—I had a hard time getting my thoughts together and even stuttered when speaking. When God called me to preach, I "reminded" Him of all this. I said "no" at first, but God's call prevailed. As it has been said, "I wouldn't give nothing for my journey right now."

God is not looking for ability, but availability. Can

God use you? Are you flexible enough to do anything He asks? Do not figure things out. Just accept the call. Be a leader and be encouraged.

Amazed By Grace

From the fullness of his grace we have all received one blessing after another.
—John 1:16

John, the writer of the fourth Gospel, was greatly amazed by grace. It was surely amazing to him that the Son of God, full of holiness and truth, loved so much as to come and dwell with a depraved humanity. Yet, what probably struck him deeply was not simply that Christ did it, but the manner in which he did.

I have come to experience something. The closer I get to the Lord, the more I hate sin and wrongdoing—both in others and in myself. It is to the point that some things disturb me and I simply shake my head. Yet, what must it have been like for Jesus?

Jesus came as the embodiment of everything right and true. Yet, he never sported an attitude about it. He never shook his head. Jesus had every right to be offended, but was not. Instead of being full of offense, he was full of grace. What a wonderful thought!

Be encouraged.

God's Tithe

"Woe to you, teachers of the law and Pharisees, you hypocrites! You give a tenth of your spices– mint, dill and cummin. But you have neglected the more important matters of the law– justice, mercy and faithfulness. You should have practiced the latter, without neglecting the former. —Matthew 23:23

In the passage above, Jesus refers to tithing. He chided the religious leaders of his day for practicing it as only a ritual and for neglecting its fuller implications. You may ask, how is tithing related to justice, mercy, and faithfulness?

The tithe was an honor given to a father or priest as unto God. (see Lev. 27:30; Deuteronomy. 26:12) In other words, as these men forsook secular employment to serve the LORD as intercessors and teachers, God supplied for their needs through the tithe.

God used His tithe also to feed those in need. In Deuteronomy 26:12 it reads: "in the year of the tithe, you shall give it to the Levite, the [visitor], the orphan and the widow, so that they may eat in your towns and be satisfied." The tithe provides for a manner of God's mercy.

God also used the tithe to teach His people reverence. In Deuteronomy 14:23, God gives instructions for the tithe so that the people might "learn to revere the LORD [their] God always." This is what this means: when you give the tithe, you give back to God what He gave to you. This helps remind us that all that we have is His and He is our everlasting supplier.

May this understanding help you to "remember the LORD your God" and to be fulfilled as a faithful steward of His blessing.

It's Time

"Rise up; this matter is in your hands. We will support you, so take courage and do it." —Ezra 10:4

It's time. Stop resting your fate on talking about the things you ought to do. Cease complaining and making excuses. Bear down and do what you need to do to get where you need to be in life. The walk of faith to which God calls you will involve conflict, hard times and diligent work. It will require you to be more flexible than you want to be. But, whatever it takes, it is time for you to rise.

Stop beating around the bush and get to it! The "matter is in your hands." You will receive support as you need it. "Take courage" and do what you need to do. God's call is too important. There will be no excuse for taking His Word lightly.

You are not too slow, too old, too young, too unhealthy, too weak, too oppressed, too helpless, or too hurt. There are no excuses. Your life is given to your charge and no one else's. You and you alone will give an account before the Lamb of God that was slain and yet lives. (Rev. 21) Take the mantle. Climb the mountain. Do not get weary. Suck it up and do it.

Rise up. It's time.

Avoid Distraction

Preach the Word; be prepared in season and out of season; correct, rebuke and encourage—with great patience and careful instruction. —2 Timothy 4:2

The Bible teaches us to be prepared to move in all situations whenever God prompts us. In the military, there is a curious principle taught: hurry up and wait. Soldiers are trained early not to hesitate whenever an order goes forth. Indeed, they teach them that every order from the commanding officer or sergeant carries weightiness and urgency. They must be quick to do it, even if they have to stand patiently after the order is completed.

This principle is a principle of authority and spiritual purpose. God's authority is absolute, but not absolutely self-serving. Our destiny is dependent on His leadership.

Our joy comes when we are instant—quick to respond to the leading of the Lord. At first, this may seem hard to do and it may be frustrating. But, there is great joy in acknowledging God's authority and knowing He can "do exceedingly abundantly above all we can ask or think." He is worthy of our immediate obedience. Anything less is an affront to Him and the great purpose He put in us.

Be encouraged.

Getting Ready for the Battle

This is the generation that seeks him, that seeks thy face, O God of Jacob. —Psalm 24:6 (KJV)

God has special plans for the youth of this generation. There is a great harvest field in the church waiting to be transformed into a harvest force.

If you want to get in the middle of the move of God, start reaching out to young people. This new generation is a generation of destiny. God is raising many awesome and excellent leaders for Christ. These young people are both in our churches and without churches to belong. They are hungry for purpose and a mission. God wants to use their strength and energy to reach nations.

I encourage you today to find a young person to mentor, to help, to reach out. Being in their lives takes time, effort and sometimes blood and sweat. But they are worth it.

Be encouraged.

Getting More Out of the Day

Trust in the Lord with all your heart and lean not on your own understanding; in all your ways acknowledge him, and he will make your paths straight. —Proverbs 3:5-6

George Mueller, a great man of faith, once said, "one can get more done with one hour of prayer and four hours of work, than with five hours of work." This is a powerful principle and, I believe, in direct obedience to the Scripture.

God wants us to lean on Him. If we pray, God will orchestrate things in a way so that we can do more things with less time and effort. I have personally watched Him put people in place, cause resources to appear, and move obstacles aside—things that would ordinarily require much time and effort.

We must learn to trust in His name. As we trust Him, He requires us to see our limitations plainly. Instead of trying to do so much, we should bring more of our business to Him on a daily basis in prayer.

We must stop killing ourselves, doing the work of four or five people in our own strength. Rather, we must show more diligence to itemizing and organizing our prayer life to bring it before God. If we trust Him and acknowledge Him in a systematic way, He will get things out of our way and make our paths straight.

Be encouraged today.

Loving Jesus

"If you love me, you will obey what I command." —John 14:15

Is everything in your life wrapped up in loving Jesus? Do you really want to know him more powerfully and intimately? When all is said and done, you will find that the Christian life is nothing but loving Jesus.

Our motivation for obeying God's commandments should not be because He will punish us. While in the world, a person is a slave to sin. Circumstances, pressures, peers, and lusts drive him or her like a slave-driver. God does not save us to become our heavenly taskmaster. He wants us to obey His instructions because we are amazed and inspired by His love that gives us free will and, by that, the option not to obey.

When we love Jesus, we have promptings inwardly to please him. It is not just what we do, it is how we do it. We go the extra mile. We give our best. We try to imitate his character.

Let love be your chief motivator and be encouraged.

The Wealth of Glory

But when He, the Spirit of truth, comes, he will guide you into all truth. He will not speak on his own; he will speak only what he hears, and he will tell you what is yet to come. —John 16:13

There is a wealth of glory that lies in the truth. We realize the value of God's glory when we submit to the truth, no matter how hard it is to take.

Truth is spiritual, not intellectual or emotional. We do not see truth through philosophy and we cannot simply "feel" something to be true. Truth spans all dimensions of life and can only be touched spiritually—in other words, we must know it by our spirit. (Prov. 20:27)

When we come to the truth, we come to Jesus. As the Word of God made flesh, Jesus states in John 17:17, "sanctify them by the truth; Thy word is truth." The word of God will never fail or pass away, even if heaven and earth pass away. Thus, it is truth. As we come see Jesus, we realize the wealth of glory.

The wealth of glory is what God has for us as we walk with Him. By His wonderful grace, God canceled our debt as believers in Christ. We will no longer face the punishment we deserve. But, by the riches of His grace and glory, God also provides us a great inheritance and spiritual authority. We may know that God has supplied everything we need for the fullness of joy, peace and all goodness as we walk in His way.

Be encouraged!

Personal Discipline

I no longer call you servants, because a servant does not know his master's business. Instead, I have called you friends, for everything that I learned from my Father I have made known to you. —John 15:15

The kingdom of God is a business. When God first created Adam, He gave him responsibility in the kingdom business to "tend to" the earth. Adam was to establish and maintain order in God's earthly creation. God made him a junior partner in His divine enterprise.

In the passage above, Jesus is speaking to mature disciples. He is speaking to men that he had trained for three years. Acknowledging their maturity ("I no longer call you servants"), Jesus promotes them to junior partners in his Kingdom work. This is the place for a mature believer.

In Christian maturity, we reach a point of understanding the business of being about business. Our relationship to our church is purposeful. We understand our role in the body and are diligent in fulfilling it. We no longer need motivation from others; our motivation comes directly out of our passion to serve the Lord. We have a sense of fulfillment that comes from the fact that we have been honored and entrusted with an important task in the kingdom, and we are doing it.

Do not settle for being simply servants. Know that God has an important place for you in the kingdom and greatly expects for you to step up into it. Seek maturity in God.

Be encouraged.

To the Name!

And rejoice before the Lord your God at the place he will choose as a dwelling for his Name– you, your sons and daughters, your menservants and maidservants, the Levites in your towns, and the aliens, the fatherless and the widows living among you. —Deuteronomy 16:11

Blessed be the Name of the Lord! The Name of the Lord is holy. It is the expression of His character. God came to Abraham as El Shaddai ("Almighty God") and El Elyon ("God of gods"). When He met Moses at the burning bush, He introduced His eternal Name, YHWH—translated Yahweh or Jehovah ("I AM"). Our culture has lost the significance of the name. We are more concerned with how it sounds or whether it rhymes, than what it means. But, as we come to know God, I believe we must also know the power that is in His name.

Think of it like this: many can remember the dramatic photograph of three or four soldiers hoisting up a flag under great duress. With great risk to their lives, these brave Marines fought with great vigilance to erect the United States flag on the Japanese island of Iwo Jima. More than 4,000 soldiers lost their lives and well over 15,000 were wounded for this to be done. Why? Because if a flag is erected over enemy territory that territory has been taken.

We must with the same diligence, uphold the Name of God in our hearts and lives. It is the Name that matters, and not our own lives. Let the very territory in our hearts be conquered for God and "take every thought captive to Christ." Be encouraged.

To Live is Christ

For to me, to live is Christ and to die is gain. —Philippians 1:21

Our single motivation as believers is Christ. Every other motivation is distraction. Eventually, we will enter the fullness of eternity. When we see His face, we will worship Him in His glory forever. The beauty of His glory will completely enthrall us. The reality of this fact should impact our lives now.

Paul said, "For to me, to live is Christ." Paul spoke this out of His revelatory experience with God. He came to know the reality of salvation. Salvation was not simply "Eternal Life Insurance" for him. Salvation was sharing in communion with the one true and living God. Our Lord Jesus explained eternal life in this way: "Now this is eternal life: that they may know you, the only true God, and Jesus Christ, whom you have sent" (John 17:3). Salvation is not going to heaven but is being with God.

I pray that this truth may transform our lives. It is easy to become focused on or enthralled by our marriages, jobs, friendships, or ministry. These things are important, but our heart belongs not to them but to Christ. As we love Him and serve Him, all other things will be added.

Be Encouraged.

Encouragement

For everything that was written in the past was written to teach us, so that through endurance and the encouragement of the Scriptures we might have hope. —Romans 15:4

We all go through something sometimes. There are many avenues through which discouragement may enter our lives. Yet, God did not leave us without provision and hope. We may find encouragement in His Word.

There is nothing new under the sun. We are not alone in our times of suffering, nor are we the only ones that have ever gone through what we face sometimes. The power over suffering is the power of endurance and the power of endurance is hope. Hope, in turn, is the ability to see ourselves coming out of our personal dark times.

The blessing of the Scriptures is this: when we read them, we come face to face with God's love and power as it has operated in the lives of people. As we read the testimony of the Scriptures, they enliven our own testimony of God's faithfulness. When we are assured of God's love and grace in our lives, we have hope.

May you have hope today. A man once said: "A man can go weeks without food; he can go days without water; a man can even go minutes without breathing air. But, no one can live one second without hope."

Be encouraged.

What is Being Saved?

He chose to give us birth through the word of truth, that we might be a kind of first-fruits of all he created. —James 1:18

When I first came to Christ, I was unsure of the many terms used by Christians to describe what had happened. They told me I was "saved" and my natural and immediate question was, "saved from what?" I believed there was a Hell and was glad for the assurance that I was not going there, but I knew there was more.

I believe there are many of us who could ask the same or a similar question that I did when I first came to the Lord. We know that our relationship with Christ means so very much, but expressing how this is so can be difficult. What is the meaningfulness of our salvation? How do we express this?

The bottom line is that God has saved us from deception, confusion, depression, destruction and the like. He has saved us from sin and the death it brings. He has called us into undaunted truth, where we may see and respond to things as they are . . . and overcome. God's gospel is a word of truth that brings us into a truth that makes us free. Free from what? From guilt, shame, self-abasement, faulty living and the list goes on.

Glory in the truth of salvation. It may be hard to look at sometimes. But, the glory of the freedom it brings is worth it. Be encouraged.

Lift Your Prayer

"When my life was ebbing away, I remembered you, Lord, and my prayer rose to you, to your holy temple. —Jonah 2:7

There have been times when I have experienced what has been like a roller coaster ride in my heart. Quick highs and languishing lows have been the story. As I have thought about my life, there have been so many things I have wished were changed for the better. One week I struggled even to read my Bible and to pray. Like Jonah in the statement above, "My life was ebbing away. . . ."

We may endure when things get tough and we feel like we have ourselves together. However, when we come to see our personal failings in the midst of our unwanted circumstances, it is a hard pill to swallow. When we think about our lives in these terms, it is so tempting to draw back from God.

God never wants us to draw back! He wants us to press into His presence, with our mess and all, and to seek His face. Feelings of unworthiness must not stop us. Doubts must not stop us. Do not stop to deal with shame or doubt in your walk with God. Use every bit of energy you have to press into Him with praise, worship, prayer and fasting.

We are never worthy of His grace, but He is always worthy of our praise! If we walk in this by faith, God will cleanse our hearts and cover our transgressions. (Ps. 103:9-12)

Be encouraged.

The One Thing Lacking

Jesus answered, "If you want to be perfect, go, sell your possessions and give to the poor, and you will have treasure in heaven. Then come, follow me." —Matthew 19:20-21

A man who because of his faithfulness to God, suffered and died under Nazi persecution once said, "When Christ calls you, he calls you to come and die." The dying here is more profound than just ending up in a grave. Dying is forsaking yourself for something greater. It is throwing everything else aside to be obedient to the plain and simple words of Jesus. There is no lesser calling and, indeed, nothing less will answer that yearning in our spirit.

This is what Jesus calls us to do. He wants us to "sell" everything that we hold dear on this earth and follow him without hesitation. How hard is this? Seemingly, it is the hardest thing to do in the world. Yet, we must consider that He promises "you will have treasure in heaven." It is more than "pie in the sky by and by." Jesus is saying, "I will employ you in the greatest work of your life and pay you in an eternal currency." How I pray that we may see this and give him all.

Be encouraged.

Claim the Harvest

The children born during your bereavement will yet say in your hearing, 'This place is too small for us; give us more space to live in.' —Isaiah 49:20

In the Kingdom of God there is calling and then there is coordination. There is the mission, but then there is the assignment. Our calling and mission is to reach the nations of the earth with the Gospel of Christ. But, in every generation and in every season, there is a specific way in which this is done.

God has a plan. He has a way for us to reach the nations. He has direction so that we can be effective and come along side Him in the work. God has ordained us to reap a harvest and this harvest is among our children.

In churches here in the United States and in other nations, there is a massive population of young people. Some of them have impactful relationships with Christ, many of them do not—but they are there. These are children of covenant. They are children of blessing, under the covering of the church. Yet, they are untapped and often unreached.

This harvest among young people is untapped. We must claim the harvest. If this generation is engaged and empowered for ministry, they will be the mightiest force in the move of the Gospel the world has ever seen. Do you believe this?

Be encouraged.

Keeping Score

*In everything that he undertook in the ser-
vice of God's temple and in obedience to
the law and the commands, he sought his
God and worked wholeheartedly. And so
he prospered. —2 Chronicles 31:21*

When we sit around the family table with our
favorite board game, everyone plays for fun and
plays to win. There may be one person holding the
pen and pad, but everyone keeps score throughout
the game. We usually do not simply play to play; as
we play, we work at our score.

We must practice keeping score our lives. In this
extremely hectic world, be careful with your commitments. For when you get involved in something,
you should be diligent and watch carefully that you
are being productive in the right things.

Do not just aimlessly walk about. Stick to the mission and keep score. Be encouraged.

Praying the Lord of the Harvest

Ask the Lord of the harvest, therefore, to send out workers into his harvest field.
—Matthew 9:38

Prayer is the essential element of ministry. Ministry without prayer is simply casual service. What we do without praying may seem effective, but ultimately it does not last.

In the general sense of the word, everything that we do should be ministry. Husbands should minister to their wives and vice versa. Christians should minister to others with whom they are in relationship, whether it is home, church, school, job, etc.. Every task we undertake should, in the general sense, be a ministry.

How do you know when work overloads you? You are beyond your limits when you cannot cover your work in prayer. If you cannot stay before the Lord and beseech his favor concerning this or that work, beware of committing yourself to it.

God does not call us into the work of the harvest to stress us out. He calls us to pray as well so that the needs of the Harvest and the work can be met by His strength and not yours. Be encouraged.

Secrets to Prayer

*The watchman replies, "Morning is com-
ing, but also the night. If you would ask,
then ask; and come back yet again."*
—Isaiah 21:12

This passage refers to a nation that faced trouble. As they looked for hope, they were told that things would get better. However, things only got worse. Many of us can identify with this, yet there is cause for encouragement nonetheless.

The word of the Lord calls us to ask. God calls us to call on Him. He has not promised us an easy road—this we know. Yet, as we go through our dark nights and brightening days, we can find shelter and comfort in Him.

The Father wants us to ask and, then, ask again. Keep seeking His word for perspective and revelation. He enjoins us to come to Him over and again to get what we need for the moment.

If your life shutters in the cool of night, pray to the Father in Christ and you will have peace. (Phil. 4:6) And should your fortune be in the light of day, do not forget to pray. Rather remember night is coming again and He wants you to be ready. Be encouraged.

Groaning

Not only so, but we ourselves, who have the firstfruits of the Spirit, groan inwardly as we wait eagerly for our adoption as sons, the redemption of our bodies.
—Romans 8:23

As the Holy Spirit regenerates our hearts, we gain a refreshed and newly empowered conscience. You can be sure you are a child of God if in your daily walk, you are quickly and often convicted of sin. This conviction is not a sign that you are further away from God; it shows that you are getting closer and closer.

Conviction causes groaning in our spirits. The Holy Spirit, who resides in us, helps us to know inwardly those things in our lives not pleasing to God. Be careful not to forsake the groaning, for this is easy to do. We can become enraptured in other things and drawn away from this inward churning.

Beloved, be aware of God's leading and His Holy Spirit's prompting. Be careful not to let your feelings overrule your faith and faithfulness to God. The groanings are there to help to press into the glory. Claim what is really important, my friends, and be encouraged.

Never Admit Defeat

My eyes have seen the defeat of my adversaries; my ears have heard the rout of my wicked foes. —Psalm 92:11

There is power is positive confession, but this principle has its weaknesses and limitations. Many of us have been disappointed because with everything in us we have tried to stay positive in a situation only for things to end miserably. Hearts broken from this kind of experience are hard to mend.

How do we persevere through tough times when it seems like we are completely powerless? How do we avoid the notion that "there's nothing I can do to change it so I have just got to accept it?" Never, never, never admit defeat.

David, the poet-warrior-king, faced discouragement on most levels. It is not hard to show that at times he felt like giving up on life. But, he encouraged himself in the Lord. He did not encourage himself with pithy confessions or positive thinking. He chased after God in prayer and through praise and worship. When he found Him, God lifted up his head.

Never, never, never admit defeat. If you have gone as far as you can go, go further anyway. Press into God's presence and He will show you defeat—not of you, but of your Enemy.

Be encouraged.

Authority and Prayer

Then God said, "Let us make man in our image, in our likeness, and let them rule..."
—Genesis 1:26

Why does it seem God needs us to pray? Why does He clearly and so regularly hold back His hand waiting for our request? If God already knows what we need, why do we need to pray? Do our prayers change things or do they simply change us?

The fact is, our prayers bring about great rewards and great victories. Prayer is a practice of releasing the grace and provision of God. Put simply, God in His divine wisdom and knowledge knows what we, His children, need even before we seem to need it. (Ps. 139:4; Isa. 46:10; Matthew 6:7-8) He has already provided for the answer in heaven, but He will not give it until we ask. Why? Because He has put the things here on earth in our hands. He will not bypass the order He has established or nullify our responsibility.

God's power and grace are readily available to bold, fervent, persistent prayer warriors who are ready and willing to take their rightful authority in Christ's name on the earth. As all authority in heaven and earth are Christ's, we can go to the Father in His name and receive whatever power we need to live out the life of Christ in the earth. Great are the rewards of faithful prayers, beloved, and great is our God.

Be encouraged.

Praying Things Through

During that long period, the king of Egypt died. The Israelites groaned in their slavery and cried out, and their cry for help because of their slavery went up to God.
—Exodus 2:23

A clear and well-founded principle in Scripture is that God's promises are always sure. Yet, there is also mounting evidence that most times His promises come to pass only at the point that we seek Him.

I have learned that God is Sovereign and in control, but He has left us in charge in this world. We have a charge to keep and God will not contradict His will in this.

For instance, God delivered the children of Abraham, Isaac and Israel after 430 years from bondage to the Egyptians (Ex. 12:40). Yet, He had promised that their bondage needed only be 400 years (Gen. 15) This means that they spend an extra thirty years longer than was needed.

There will be times of adversity for each of us. You may be going through this right now Yet, we must learn to be prayerful in these times. Do not allow your troubles to drive you from God! Pray things through lest you find yourself in your mess longer than you need to be.

Be encouraged.

Answers

"Answer me, O Lord, answer me, so these people will know that you, O Lord, are God, and that you are turning their hearts back again." —1 King 18:37

Answers are the keys to success in one's prayer life. They fuel passion in prayer and keep praying people praying.

Our relationship with God is to be real and personal. If we base our life with God simply on theological principles, then we are to be pitied indeed. If we only count on conjectures and finding meaning in interesting circumstances, then we are playing games with ourselves. For us to know that God is God, we must have answers to prayer.

When I gave my life to the Lord, it was contingent upon Him answering me. I needed to know the Giver of the Word was alive and well. I did not get a fantastical, earthshaking answer; but, God answered me. In fact, He will answer anyone who with faith and patience is willing to seek Him. (Rom. 10:13) Be encouraged to seek the answers.

Keeping the Faith

I have fought the good fight, I have finished the race, I have kept the faith. Now there is in store for me the crown of righteousness, which the Lord, the righteous Judge, will award to me on that day– and not only to me, but also to all who have longed for his appearing. —2 Timothy 4:7-8

Prayer is the ultimate act of faith. Without a prayer life, there is no real spiritual life. If we are to "keep the faith," we must set out heart to pray unceasingly.

Is your prayer life a burden to you? Surely this should not be, but in truth it is for so many sincere believers. We know we should pray more, but we simply do not. Beloved, if your prayer life is weak, it is likely that your focus is off.

Prayer is an act of entering into the work of God, while ceasing from your labor. (John 6:29; Heb. 4:9-11) Practically speaking, it is "stepping into Christ's shoes" and fulfilling his life and work on the earth. The connection that occurs in prayer makes this possible.

When you pray, are you seeking God to do your will or are you seeking to fulfill His calling? Are your desires about things that are fleeting and temporal or eternal and lasting? Keep the faith and be encouraged.

P-U-S-H

So Ahab went off to eat and drink, but Elijah climbed to the top of Carmel, bent down to the ground and put his face between his knees. —1 King 18:42

Prayer is not an obligation or duty. Prayer is a process. It is the regular flow of the vibrant spiritual life. It is not something outward influences drive us to, rather inward ones do.

I have found that every weakness in my prayer life stems from a wrong understanding of what prayer is. By praying according to my own will and sense of duty, I have forfeited many answers. Instead, my sense of need and spiritual desire should have driven me. The principle is simple: When we are hungry, we will do whatever it takes to be filled.

Answers come when we are willing to PUSH: "Pray Until Something Happens." We will sometimes need to travail like a woman birthing a child, or as symbolically shown by Elijah on Mt. Carmel. (1 Ki. 18: 42) This kind of persistence comes from rich desire, not simply strong commitment. "Set your heart on things above" (cp. Matt. 6:21; Col. 3:1) and do not let go of the promise until God blesses you!

Be encouraged.

Prayer for the Persecuted

Remember those in prison as if you were their fellow prisoners, and those who are mistreated as if you yourselves were suffering. —Hebrews 13:3

One role of intercession is to come alongside the suffering and to carry their burden away through prayer. We must begin to let our hearts be touched and tied to the heart of others who are suffering—especially if they suffer for the cause of Christ. We must cry and cry out with them and let God hear our united voice.

Christians are suffering persecution all over the world. Do your research. Read their story and let your heart reach out to theirs. I encourage you today, let your passion be set afire for deliverance of the persecuted today.

Getting it All Done

All his days his work is pain and grief; even at night his mind does not rest. This too is meaningless. —Ecclesiastes 2:23

We succeed not by the works of our hands, but by walking in faith and seeing God's work on our behalf. When we work alone, without His guidance and help, we work vanity. "Unless the Lord build the house, they labor in vain that build it" (Ps. 127). God does not mean for the labor of our lives to be vanity. He means for us to get things done in the wake of His grace.

There are some exertions that are good for us while others are definitely bad. When we exercise, we press ourselves to the limit ultimately to produce greater strength and fitness. On the other hand, we can stress ourselves into a heart-attack or stroke when we press on without wisdom. In life we should strain. The issue is how will we deal with it when it comes.

We all have the strain of getting it all done. Yet, we do not all use wisdom in doing so. By wisdom, we become flexible and we can adjust. By wisdom, we do not have to have everything now and we learn how to sacrifice the unnecessary, time-consuming things of life. By wisdom, we become creative, yet focused.

God grants wisdom to those who ask. Know this and be encouraged.

Helpful Wisdom

A man finds joy in giving an apt reply– and how good is a timely word! —Proverbs 15:23

Seek earnestly to be an encourager. There is so much and so many messages to discourage the human soul. One sure way to be a blessing is to provide encouragement to others. I have felt for a long time that, instead of tracts, encouragement cards would be much more effective in witnessing.

"An anxious heart weighs a man down, but a kind word cheers him up" (Prov. 12:25). Seek to give without concern for receiving. Be pleased in the good pleasure of others and do not fear someone taking advantage of you. With this attitude, you will always be ready for an apt word at the right moment.

God has blessed you and given you wisdom from above. Take this blessing and bless someone else. Practice that art of uplifting and get good at it.

Be encouraged.

Faith and Miracles

*He could not do any miracles there, except
lay his hands on a few sick people and heal
them. —Mark 6:5*

How is it possible that the Bible should read that
Jesus "could not do" something? This is a troubling
and difficult fact. Yet, as with all truth, our understanding this will be liberating.

Miracles still happen. Many of us have been
taught to doubt this. On one side, they teach us a so-
called "healthy skepticism." On the other, we are
spoiled by extravagant counterfeit signs and wonders. By either means, we become offended at
Christ.

Offense is the source of the unbelief that blocks us
from experiencing God's miraculous power.
Miracles are one of God's gifts to the Body. (1 Cor.
12:8-11) In perspective, they are not "sideshows,"
but aids in the preaching of the Gospel. (Matt. 12:39;
1 Cor. 2:4-5) Much like a hand on a human body, we
may do without them, but lose their tremendous
effectiveness. Why do without them if their use
would honor Christ?

We should be open to miracles, seek the gifting as
a Body, and trust the Lord to lead us in their use.
They likely will not be manifested in a local Body of
Christ unless there is a spirit of agreement and
togetherness. (Matt. 18:19) Let us free ourselves

from offense and trust the Lord to work as He would please among us. Let future generations not record of us, "And he did not do many miracles there because of *their* lack of faith" (Matt. 13:58; *italics mine*)

Be encouraged.

The Blessings of Eden

The Lord God took the man and put him in the Garden of Eden to work it and take care of it. —Genesis 2:15

There were many blessings in the Garden. There, Adam had the hope of eternal life, intimacy with God and immeasurable provision. When he and Eve fell, these blessings became only marginally accessible. Yet, in Christ, the door to the blessings of Eden is flung open wide by faith.

In the first sense, faith opens up to us the blessed hope of eternal life. We may see that our life will not end when our bodies cease to live. We may see that we have an everlasting life in which we will serve God at the level of our eternal reward. This is to say, our eternal life is free, but it will not be spent idly. We will rather we live with privileges and responsibilities that will be rewards of our faithfulness now. How piteous it will be to enjoy entrance into God's eternal kingdom and find out that we could enjoy so much more if only we had been more faithful.

Ask the question, "Am I doing what I am being paid to do?" Though our rewards in heaven ultimately come out of God's grace, here He gives them in direct response to our faithfulness.

Be encouraged.

The Move of Faith

Therefore, since we are surrounded by such a great cloud of witnesses, let us throw off everything that hinders and the sin that so easily entangles, and let us run with perseverance the race marked out for us. —Hebrews 12:1

There are two major hindrances to a move of faith among God's people. Overly structured, controlling religion beset us on the one hand and undisciplined, disorderly religious experiences on the other. God is displeased with the inflexibility of the one and the lack of moderation in the other.

Beware of becoming too dependent on church regulations. This traps our faith and comes from a lack of spiritual maturity in the Body. We must develop mature leadership who will raise mature believers and trust them to hear from God within a faithful process.

On the other hand, we must abhor lack in spiritual discipline and lapsed spiritual order. We must become mature enough to be free while avoiding silliness. We need the flexibility to respond quickly to God's move, while maintaining the integrity of Biblical order and process.

Few really understand Biblical process and the maturity it requires. We are often too skiddish to endure the challenges of life that work godly maturity in our lives. Either, we ignore the responsibilities of mature faith or we take them on without paying the price. Enough of this! Let us see these extremes for what they are and press for a more excellent way.

Living By Faith

"See, he is puffed up; his desires are not upright– but the righteous will live by his faith." —Habakkuk 2:4

What does it mean to "live by faith?" Why does this simple instruction seem so difficult for so many? It is clear that God calls us to "live by faith" and doing so produces a greater, more blessed life. Yet, so many are confused and afraid to walk in this privilege. Put this confusion to rest.

Faith is a powerful tool. By it, we have access to God's great store of gracious promises. It enables us to walk in divinely granted authority and power as we apply God's Word in our lives. Miracles happen when it is present. Answers come when it arises. Blessings follow the request made by faith. Viewing things with faith enhances life. Faith pleases God and opens our lives to many open demonstrations of His grace.

Why are so many confused about this? We get confused when we mix our faith and our lusts. (See Jas. 4:3) Living by faith does not involve wayward desires and self-aggrandizement. It is not about lust, pride and flesh. To the contrary, true faith leads away from these to godly things like "righteousness, peace and joy in the Holy Spirit" (Rom. 14:17)

Beloved, we must stop living for this world. Eternity is before us and is waiting for our hearts.

Will you not lodge your heart with the anchor of faith in eternity's flowing river? Will you not release the petty benefits this world has to offer and let heaven's everlasting blessing break forth in your life? (Matt. 19:29) Live by faith, my friends, and truly live.

Be encouraged.

Dried Up?

Then the Lord said to Abraham, "Why did Sarah laugh and say, 'Will I really have a child, now that I am old?' Is anything too hard for the Lord? I will return to you at the appointed time next year and Sarah will have a son." —Genesis 18:13-14

Beloved, God wants to use you to offer His blessings to the world. You have been placed on the earth for a purpose. God has given you gifts, talents and abilities. Be encouraged you not to give up.

God chose Abraham to be the father of many nations and a blessing to the world for generations to come (Gen. 12). He chose Sarah for this too. Yet, when Sarah laughed when she heard God would cause her to birth a son. She was long passed her child bearing years and she saw herself as "dried up."

Some of us laugh at the prospect of God using us. Past failure and wounds make us feel "dried up." You are not the first to feel this way. Moses felt dried up too. He sought and failed to be a deliverer for his people and was "hung out to dry" for forty years in the wilderness. Elijah worked great miracles in his prime, but failed to turn the hearts of the people back to God. He ended up "dried up" under a tree ready to die. On the fateful night they captured Christ, Peter rose to defend him. The Lord stayed his hand.

Confused and bewildered, Peter "dried up" so much he denied the One for whom he had earlier risked his life.

You may have tried God and seemingly failed, but do not give up. Do not laugh in derisiveness and doubt. God will yet enliven your spiritual womb and you will deliver His great purpose that He placed in you. I know He will.

Be encouraged.

Fresh Anointing

Make these into a sacred anointing oil, a fragrant blend, the work of a perfumer. It will be the sacred anointing oil. —Exodus 30:25

It is not necessary for God to refresh the anointing on our lives. By definition, an anointing is done only once. Yet, we do need a fresh anointing. We need to keep it fresh.

The anointing is a sacred covering that sets us apart for God's use. As He marks us for special use, God grants us the right to handle His blessings and promises. This is the power of the anointing. It gives us access to the holy blessings of God.

Since God shares access to His holy things—His blessings, His answers to prayer, the authority in His Name—we must keep the anointing fresh and unspoiled. Let us not let ourselves get mixed in with the stench of this world. Let us avoid selfish desire and spoiling pleasures. Let us endeavor always to keep fresh the fragrance of God's Spirit for His pleasure and for the lost.

The anointing of God is upon you. Keep it fresh and be encouraged.

The Threat of Failure

You know, brothers, that our visit to you was not a failure. —1 Thessalonians 2:1

It is one thing to fail and a completely different one to face the *threat* of failure. The threat of failure is a plague that attacks our faith when we need it most. It is the downside of taking a necessary risk. Invariably when we step out or try something new, a period of doubt and fear comes. This experience was not foreign to Paul the apostle.

God called Paul to step out into something completely new. Paul's message of salvation through faith in Christ and the unification of the Jews and Gentiles was not only new, but risky business. Paul was whipped, beaten and wounded for it. Paul also had to worry whether the foundation of the gospel that he laid was going to hold. He was suffering and striving hard without being able to see the fruit of his labor.

In the face of possible failure, Paul trusted in the one who called him. He rested in the fact that God chose him and that God would shore up whatever was left undone. Paul wrote to one church, "[I am] confident of this, that he who began a good work in you will carry it on to completion until the day of Christ Jesus" (Phil. 1:6) Paul understood that God was working as he worked. In fact, he could only do what he was doing because God was doing what He was doing.

You cannot make it without God in anything. Take comfort in God during tough times and know that He will complete the work He began with and in you. Be encouraged.

Be a Bold Witness

*"But you will receive power when the
Holy Spirit comes on you; and you will be
my witnesses in Jerusalem, and in all
Judea and Samaria, and to the ends of the
earth." —Acts 1:8*

When we firmly decide to do God's work, we step
out into a new thing. Being a witness means that we
are challenging things the way that they are. Listen
to what Peter said in his first sermon in Acts 2:40—
"With many other words he warned them; and he
pleaded with them, 'Save yourselves from this cor-
rupt generation.'"

To be employed by God is to walk as light in darkness. There is no room for compromise. We must
believe and live by either God's truth or the world's
perversion of truth. Of course, it is hard to live in the
world by God's truth. Jesus made this crystal clear,
"All men will hate you because of me," and goes on
to say, "but he who stands firm to the end will be
saved" (Mark 13:13).

It is hard to live by God's truth because the world
refuses to acknowledge it. The world cannot and will
not see spiritual things. Yet, trust is rooted in the
realm of the spirit. In spite of all this, God promised
that as we stand boldly on the truth of God, He
would give us power to be His witnesses and prove
His perfect will through our lives.

Stand on the truth and never feel defenseless. You never have to convince anyone of it. Rather know the nature of truth is to be self-evident and God Himself will defend it (see Prov. 2:20-31). Be encouraged!

Standing on God's Word

*So then, brothers, stand firm and hold to
the teachings we passed on to you,
whether by word of mouth or by letter.
—2 Thessalonians 2:15*

So much of what we do in the body of Christ is of
the flesh. God has said, "Then the LORD said, 'My
Spirit will not contend (rule over, compel) with man
forever, for he is mortal; his days will be a hundred
and twenty years'" (Gen. 6:3). We do so much out of
our mortal limitations and the strength of the flesh.
God does not bless our work as we do this. God only
blesses the work of those that operate by His Word.

There is so much that God wants to speak to us
through His Word, the Bible. When we take the time
to engage it, He will give us specific direction for our
daily living. Now, we are not inwardly inclined to
follow God way. We are brought to this by applying
His Word to our lives. Again I say, God's instruction
is not natural to us. We must adjust our lives to do
what He says.

God's Word is like a stairway before us. Each
word of instruction and direction and guidance is a
new step in front of us. We must make some adjust-
ment and apply some effort to stand on the next step,
but each step takes us higher. Do not be a hearer of
the Word and not a doer. This is harmful and foolish.

Be encouraged, dear friends.

Chasing God's Heart

He testified concerning him: "I have found David son of Jesse a man after my own heart; he will do everything I want him to do." —Acts 13:22

God is looking for souls that will chase His heart. He wants intimacy with His children. He wants to teach us to have a pure heart and a pure faith. Great things will He do with the one who rises before the sun to give glory to His name.

There are times it seems God does not answer our prayers. Do not be discouraged. Have faith! Sometimes God's silence is a call to deeper intimacy. He wants our prayers in more earnest.

God is looking for a faith that brings true intimacy. He is looking for one who will seek Him no matter what. He has more for us than we imagine, if we would only seek Him with all our hearts.

Hear His call for you to draw near to His heart. Cross every boundary to meet Him in His limitless love and power.

Be encouraged.

The Secret of Sanctification

You did not choose me, but I chose you and appointed you to go and bear fruit– fruit that will last. Then the Father will give you whatever you ask in my name. —John 15:16

Our Father is not impressed with good works. Great discipline does not impress Him. These things are good in some respects, but they are not what draw us closer to his heart.

God is looking for a soul that will respond with immediacy to His voice. Peter, James and John made up Christ's innermost circle. When Jesus called, the Bible says, "straightway they left their nets and followed him" (Mark 1:16-20) They were close because responded with immediacy to his voice.

It is good to rise early to read your Bible or pray. Praise God for the men and women that labor many long hours in prayer. Those that boldly share their faith do well. But, works do not impress God. He is pleased by the attitude behind such diligence. It is the ear to hear his call and the heart to respond with immediacy that pleases God. (Phil. 2:12-13)

Work at responding ever more readily to the Spirit's call and be encouraged.

When God Opens Doors

Now when I went to Troas to preach the gospel of Christ and found that the Lord had opened a door for me...
—2 Corinthians 2:12

If we want open doors in our lives, we must go. Jesus commanded his disciples, as recorded my Matthew, to "Go ye therefore . . ." and he then promised "I will be with you." (Matt. 28:18-20) This commission stands for us today and so does the promise.

Many of us are waiting for God to do something before we go. Some of us are waiting for God to speak to us. We want a specific word or prompting. We are waiting for God to speak to us when He was already spoken in His Word!

We will never see God truly with us and working in our lives consistently until we go. No matter whether it is to the nursing homes, the streets, college campuses, our families, overseas missions, or whatever, we will be out of order with God until we go. But, when we go . . .

Be encouraged.

Maximize the Moment

Let your moderation be known to all men.
—Ephesians 4:5 (KJV)

The issue of maximizing the moment has long been a major issue in the history of the church. The early saints chiefly advocated it in the virtue of simplicity. Every notable ancient saint heavily pursued the great things of God through simplicity.

Life becomes so complicated and our thoughts so jumbled. Simplicity calls us to examine our limitations and to be assertive about not letting our plate get too full. It calls us to acknowledge the world God has created around us and to recognize that we are only part of it.

This world's weight is not on our shoulders and we are not accountable to see to everything getting done. Simplicity calls us to know our part, play our part with passion and really, really trust God to do the rest.

Find the beauty of simplicity. By this, we may maximize the moments God has given us. We become so busy with things to do and there is only one thing necessary.

When you see God in glory, you will realize something. You will behold the beauty of His holiness. You will lose composure like the angels of heaven who perpetually shout, "Holy, Holy, Holy." You will look at your Father and Savior and Lord in

His glory and you will say with awe-inspired tears, "All I ever wanted was You."

I encourage you to start learning this lesson now

Indefensible Faith?

. . . His truth shall be your shield and buckler. —Psalm 91:4 (KJV)

Your relationship with Christ is not a religion. It is not a "belief-of-choice." You did not choose Christ. He chose you.

The testimony of Christ is not a myth or a good moral story. It is historical fact, present-day reality, and future confirmation. No one can deny that Jesus Christ lived, died by crucifixion, and rose from the dead. He is alive and impacting lives today. Current events strongly point to the prophecy of his return. The life, death, resurrection and return of Christ is truth, gospel truth.

Truth is true whether it convinces us or not. We do not need to defend the truth, only to declare it. The truth will defend itself by its own virtue. We do not have an indefensible faith. We have a faith that needs no defense. Never let the world put you on the defensive to diminish your witness. Boldly declare the truth and let God's truth defend itself.

Having the Mind of Christ

Have this mind in you that was also in Christ Jesus. —Philippians 2:5 (KJV)

God has worked tremendous things in my life. There have been times that I lost the desire to pray. There were times when I struggled with my faith, my calling, my effectiveness. I occasionally wanted to give up. I encouraged others, but deep down had to encourage myself consistently.

Times come when it seems like our whole world is falling apart. We become like Jesus when the Spirit led him out into the wilderness to be tempted of the devil. We are hungry and not fed. We are frustrated and unhappy with our "process," and God does not answer any of our prayers for relief. We want our destiny and our calling to be fulfilled in our lives, but it seems so far off. And the devil knows it and seeks so carefully to get us to forfeit the pain and process.

I thank God that He has given me the mind not to give up or give in. I have already been through too much and God has forgiven me of too much, even when I forfeited my process. I praise Him for His mercy and steadfast love that has not let me go. And now, after my wilderness, I am experiencing angels coming to minister and I am experiencing His glory like never before.

Be encouraged.

When Do You Rest?

*By the seventh day God had finished the work
he had been doing; so on the seventh day he
rested from all his work. —Genesis 2:2*

When do you rest? Do you have a plan for spending time resting? Is everything go, go, go until you drop? This is the case for many of us in this perverse generation. Each of us learn early to press our limits. This is not God's way.

God rested on the seventh day not for Himself, but for us. "The Sabbath was made for man, not man for the Sabbath." God needed no rest, nor did He need to tell us when He took one. But, our Father provides this example for all of us.

God created us in His image, but we are limited. We can only do so much and go so far. He wants us to acknowledge our limitations by managing our time well and honoring rest. Just like the fact we should not spend more money than we have, we should not transgress the limits of time and energy. It is this debt-driven, credit-based society that drives us and gives us the illusion that we can keep going, pushing without regards to limits.

Know yourself and respect your limitations. Definitely, grow where you can. But, know you can only do so much—you are not God. Do not be deceived, God is not mocked.

Be Encouraged.

April 12

When You Don't Know Where to Go

Love . . . always trusts. —1 Corinthians 13:6,7

Many people are hurting, but they do not know where to go. We hear the words "take it to Jesus," but feel this is not enough. We believe Jesus should be enough, but the wounds fester on. This brings further shame and doubt. Yet, when God saw that Adam was alone, He did not say to Adam, "Take it to Jesus." Rather, He fashioned a bride from his side, out of the same stuff, to stand by him. God did not want him to be alone and provided a companion for him.

Beloved, God does not want us to be alone. He has someone made of the same stuff to stand with us. This may not be in terms of a mate. It may be a good friend. The relationship may be permanent or temporary. But, God will provide for you.

As you seek God and as He shows you your friend, you must lean on the merits of God's handiwork and open up. This is not an admonition to disclose your heart to everyone with a listening ear. You must come to know when God is providing for you.

God did not make you to be alone. He will supply what you need. Look for Him in those He brings your way. It could be a long-time friend or a woman at the grocery store you never met before nor will meet again. If you are hurting, God has someone for you. May this encourages you.

About Mourning

*When I wept, and chastened my soul with
fasting, that was to my reproach. —Psalm
69:10 (KJV)*

There is a time to rejoice and a time to weep, a time to laugh and a time to mourn. Bad things happen. When they happen to you, please know, God does not take pleasure in seeing this. Rather, God's heart grieves with you and for you.

God mourns and we must learn how to mourn as He does. I believe in every single thing, we must have the heart of God. Yet, too often we do not take the proper time and focus to mourn over situations and circumstances. Often we try to avoid mourning and end up dragging out the process, wounding ourselves further in the process.

In today's scripture, David—once called a man after God's own heart—chose not to ignore bad circumstances to escape them. Rather, he faced them and addressed them with fasting and prayer. The Bible says he "afflicted his soul from morning until evening" when he mourned. His mourning was definite; it had a beginning and an ending point.

I encourage you today, if there are things in your past that continue to weigh your heart, face them and set a time to mourn over them. Also, if there are circumstances or injustices around you, do not harden your heart. Take time to mourn over them with fasting and prayer and seek God to make a difference. God faces us in our sin, though it breaks His heart. Let us not be afraid to face hard things and feel hard things.

Be encouraged.

Faith Living

Set your minds on things above, not on earthly things. —Col 3:2

Faith is not simply a tool to get want we want from God. Faith is a perspective. It determines how we think about life and the issues of life. It determines what we should receive as a "given" in life. Faith is, by God's grace, seeing things from God's perspective.

The Bible teaches that are given the mind of Christ. True enough, we cannot understand everything that goes on around us, but we can have complete confidence in God's work and God's leading in our lives. Because of the mind of Christ, some things should be automatic. Witnessing should be automatic. Prayer should be automatic. Thankfulness should be automatic.

Sometimes, though we have the mind of Christ, we get bogged down in stuff. Oh, how we get bogged down! But, we can have consistent victory in Christ if we set our minds of things above. We must learn to see things in terms of heaven.

Learn how God sees you and your situations in life. You assessment of yourself may be accurate and still be untrue. You may have done what the world said you did, but you are not who the world says you are.

Be encouraged.

What Strategy?

Once again David inquired of the Lord, and the Lord answered him, "Go down to Keilah, for I am going to give the Philistines into your hand." —1 Samuel 23:4

What is your strategy in reaching the lost? Our Great Commission is like a great spiritual war being fought. What strategy are we using to see the measures of victory?

More than many churches have no perceivable strategy at all. A strategy is not an inflexible plan or intractable order of operation. Strategies in God are set to help us get to the point and avoid frivolous activity. The Bible says, "In his heart a man plans his course, but the LORD determines his steps" (Prov. 16:9). We must focus ourselves on the mission (the Great Commission) and then seek God, allowing Him to direct our steps.

The mission needs clear defining. We are to reach the unreached with the Gospel of Jesus Christ and to witness to the world His glory. With this in view, let us avoid shallow evangelism and even more shallow views of Christian living. Tie Your purpose into this mission. You will never be content until you do it.

Be encouraged.

The Business of Mission

And everyone who has left houses or brothers or sisters or father or mother or children or fields for my sake will receive a hundred times as much and will inherit eternal life. —Matthew 19:29

The message of the "prosperity for me" gospel is old, tired and out of vogue. There is no fulfillment in this message (except perversely for some of those that preach it). Yet, we must understand and tap into God's prosperity for the sake of mission.

When we give ourselves one hundred percent to mission, I believe God will bless us one hundred times over if we are ready and willing to receive it. When we step into the business of mission, we ought to develop an understanding this principle.

Unfortunately, many ministries have been established without wisdom regarding God's way of provision. Some of us have gone around God's plan and rushed right into something unprepared.

There are two principles I have found that we must learn that are foundational to the business of mission. First, we must learn moderation and modesty. (Phil. 4:5, 11-13; 1 Tim. 6:6) We must learn to manage our resources properly and how to set what we save into mission. Second, we must learn how to live out of answered prayers. God wants to give us a track record of answered prayer that will develop in us a lifestyle of dependence on him.

Let us learn balance and boldness in our mission of reaching souls for Christ. Be encouraged.

Mission Mind

I do not want you to be unaware, brothers, that I planned many times to come to you (but have been prevented from doing so until now) in order that I might have a harvest among you, just as I have had among the other Gentiles. —Romans 1:13

There is a subtle difference between what we call ministry and mission.

In much of what we call ministry, the minister is a "professional" whose faithfulness and effectiveness is measured by his "feeding the flock." The pastoral and teaching ministries are tremendously important. Yet, God purposes them to prepare the flock to reach the world. There is a problem when the needs of the flock become the bottom line.

Mission, as I am using the term, is different. Success in mission is based on the fulfillment of the Great Commission. Thus, the "feeding of the flock" and everything else in ministry is done ultimately to share God's amazing grace with the world. The blessings of ministry should not stockpile at the door of the church; they should break forth on the hearts of the nations.

Simply put, a mission mind rests not until we reach the nations. Let us remember our mission and be encouraged to fulfill it.

The Lord Reigns

*The Lord reigns forever; he has estab-
lished his throne for judgment. —Psalm
9:7*

How real is God's rule over your life to you?
There is too much lip service to this fact. From generation to generation, throughout Scripture and the
history that follows, we may see God looking for a
people who will radically serve Him with their
whole heart. Shall this be the generation?

From the mouth of Isaiah God asks us today,
"Whom have you so dreaded and feared that you
have been false to me, and have neither remembered
me nor pondered this in your hearts? Is it not
because I have long been silent that you do not fear
me" (Isa. 57:11)? Why must God stir us up day after
day to command our hearts?

Beware of the stifling of the world. Beware of
dulling pleasures and lulling excuses. Beware of
numbing fear. Fear the Lord and pursue his purposes. How much of all are you willing to give Him
to see the nations reached for Christ? Be encouraged,
my friends, like never before.

What Has God Said?

Fear the Lord your God, serve him only and take your oaths in his name.
—Deuteronomy 6:13

Have you ever felt less than spiritual? Do you struggle at times with sensing God presence, His desires or His will? Are you ever put out because you feel out of the loop with God? Many of us struggle with this at times.

The problem is likely this. Your walk is based more on what you think than what God has said. Moses found himself in this place and cried out, "Teach me your ways" (Ex. 33:13). David cried out for the same and added more, "Teach me your way; I will walk in Your truth. Unite my prayer to fear Your name" (Ps. 86:11).

Seek the Lord and hear His voice. Let your commitments be fulfilled in His name. Do not say, "I will do this or that." Rather, say "by Christ I will accomplish such and such" and "I will do so God permitting." This is not to be doubtful or tentative. Rather, "trust in the Lord and lean not to your own understanding . . . [and] acknowledge Him and He will make your paths straight" (Prov. 3:5,6).

Be encouraged.

Healthy Relationships

Do two walk together unless they have agreed to do so? —Amos 3:3

Too great an attachment to the things of this world has waylaid many a Christian commitment. Jesus says, "The one who received the seed that fell among the thorns is the man who hears the word, but the worries of this life and the deceitfulness of wealth choke it, making it unfruitful" (Matt. 13:22). Let us understand one major area that can affect our fruitfulness.

The relationships we hold have powerful sway in our lives. If they are positive, then we can expect to experience positive things. However, it is through our relationships that many of us at times find ourselves set off track.

Our relationships may be with family, close friends, co-workers or general associations. They can be collegial or romantic. No matter what the level, they have bearing on our fruitfulness.

We must learn to assess our relationships and understand how they must be kept. We may give too much importance and attention to some. Others may need to be severed. Some may need cultivation and some may need to be handled with care. God will give us the wisdom to handle each if we ask Him. (Jas. 1:4)

May we all learn to be careful with the relationships we have and allow ourselves to be in. It is a stewardship issue that we all must take seriously.

Be encouraged.

Wear the Garment Loosely

When I smiled at them, they scarcely believed it; the light of my face was precious to them. —Job 29:24

God does not call us to a foreboding, dry and somber life. Do not take yourself and your problems too seriously. Neither our accomplishments nor our pains will last eternally. The garment of life we must wear, we should wear loosely.

Know the richness of each moment. By this, you can laugh even when you are crying. God wants you to know the range of feelings, from profound sorrow to intense joy. By these, you come to know fullness and abundance in life. Yet, do not be so wrapped up in yourself you cannot feel for anything or anyone else.

Do not let your personal problems cast shadows over your life. Reject this form of pride. What you do does not determine your worth. God does. It is on this foundation that you can face each daily honestly and without shame. There is joy in the journey when you learn to wear the garment loosely.

Seize the fulness of each moment with grace.

Deceitfulness of Riches

A man who has riches without understanding is like the beasts that perish. —Psalm 49:20

The Kingdom of God suffers for a lack of understanding regarding riches. On one hand, some despise riches quoting the phrase, "the love of money is the root of evil." On the other, some are enamored by them plying, "you don't know how far I've come."

God is not enamored by riches. He owns everything and can make whatever He does not own. His attitude toward riches almost leans on indifference and is one of practicality. They neither allure Him nor please Him—they are there to be used for His purpose and His glory.

We must develop an attitude like our Father's. We need a mature mindset by which we can handle riches without them handling and controlling us. We must have a godly understanding about riches, lest we be drawn "offsides" because of ignorance.

Overcome the deceitfulness of riches and be encouraged.

Spirit and Power

The Spirit of the Lord will come upon you in power, and you will prophesy with them; and you will be changed into a different person. Once these signs are fulfilled, do whatever your hand finds to do, for God is with you. —1 Samuel 10:6-7

When you live your life by the power of the Spirit, He changes you into a different person. Has the power of the Spirit had this affect on your life?

Many of us look widely for that "something extra" in our lives. We try different jobs, different relationships, different churches, etc.. Yet, we must come to learn the contentment that comes in being in the Spirit, directly where God wants us to be right now.

We may know that a person is filled with the Spirit and faith by how they deal with the moment. There is a contentment and peace that the Spirit brings. When we are Spirit-filled, we have connection enough with God to know, even if the situation looks bad, that all things are in hand. We can then, "trust the Lord and do good" (Ps. 37:3).

Again, I ask you, are you filled with the Spirit right now? Do understand that this is not a reality by default. We must seek to be filled by the minutes and moments of our lives. We must continuously seek the infilling, just like we must continuously drink water. Are you filled today? Set your heart before the

Lord and see that you are. You cannot live out Christ's life without it.

Be encouraged.

Full of Faith and Spirit

*He was a good man, full of the Holy Spirit
and faith, and a great number of people
were brought to the Lord. —Acts 11:24*

For years, we in the Church have debated the relevance of the Holy Spirit in our lives. Some teach that the Spirit helps us in nondescript ways as we try to live the Christian life. Others see His presence in fantastical displays of emotion and energy. There was once a time when they taught that the ministry of the Spirit was unnecessary because its job was relegated to church leaders. How unfortunate.

It is time we stop arguing about the Spirit and walk after the Him. How dare we reduce the Spirit to a simple human experience, whether it be benign or charismatic? God has done the unimaginable—the unthinkable. He has sent His Spirit to dwell in us that He might change us, guide us, embolden us and strengthen us to walk as Christ walked.

It is impossible to walk after Christ, living out his life in the earth, without the help of the Holy Spirit. How often we miss this point in the rage over phenomena and spiritual experience!

Let us take the road less traveled, though dangerous it may be. Let us choose the impossible path, trust the aid of God through His Spirit to make all things possible. Put first things first. Seeking purpose before experience, live out Christ for the nations. It is time for Christ to show up in us by the power of the Spirit and in the fulness of our faith.

Be encouraged.

Vibrant Faith

*By faith Abraham, when called to go to a place he would later receive as his inheritance, obeyed and went, even though he did not know where he was going.
—Hebrews 11:8*

Vibrant faith involves great expectation for the future while making the most of right now. With an eye toward the coming fulfillment of God's promises, it follows Him in obedience cultivating every moment.

What are the implications of this for our lives? When you know what great and everlasting things God has for you, then you are less likely to risk losing them by what you do or fail to do now. We defeat the lust of the flesh by turning our hearts to incorruptible desires. We defeat the lust of the eyes by affirming that God has laid up better things for us. Our real knowledge that God's promises outweigh anything we could get by our own strength deflates our pride.

Let us spend our present moments empowered by our hope of what is to come. This is what the Scriptures means by "faith is the substance of things hoped for." Sacrifice now. Labor now. Invest your time wisely and know that God has laid up great rewards to be poured out on the coming Great Day!

Be encouraged.

Going Through Mountains

"Don't be afraid," the prophet answered. "Those who are with us are more than those who are with them." And Elisha prayed, "O Lord, open his eyes so he may see." Then the Lord opened the servant's eyes, and he looked and saw the hills full of horses and chariots of fire all around Elisha. —2 Kings 6:16-17

Often we do not see the resources God has placed around us. When mountains of trouble amass against us, we either sit paralyzed in fear or try to face the mountain in our measly strength. This is not walking by faith.

By faith, we perceive and embrace the promises of God. (Heb. 11:13) We receive the revelation of God's present provision. As we pray and seek God's face, the Bible assures us that He "will guide us with His eye" (Ps. 32:8). With this access to God's strength, we can face any mountain.

A friend has said to me, "You get the gifts from the master you serve." If you serve the god of this world, you can expect no good thing. If you serve yourself, you can expect very little. But, if you serve the God of glory, you will have "every good and perfect gift" and be able to go through every mountain—no matter how impossible it may seem. Know this and be encouraged.

The Importance of Salvation

. . . how shall we escape if we ignore such a great salvation? —Hebrews 2:3

What is the greatest result of Jesus Christ's work of salvation? Is it forgiveness? Peace? Guidance? All these are great and wonderful, but the greatest result of Christ's work was the satisfaction of his own desires.

The greatest thing about our salvation is its importance to Christ. He did not love us simply to save us from destruction. He won us for himself. He takes pleasure in the thought of us walking with him in eternal light. Jesus says through his Word to us today, "I call you friends" (see John 15:13-15).

The Lord offers us his friendship and he greatly desires ours. This is a wonderful thought.

Be encouraged.

The Purpose of Power

But I have raised you up for this very pur-
pose, that I might show you my power and
that my name might be proclaimed in all
the earth. —Exodus 9:16

The sureness of our faith lies in the hands of God. (1 Cor. 2:4-5) His Word of power is our foundation. We serve a God of power and His kingdom "is not a matter of talk but of power" (1 Cor. 4:20). He shows His power both with an outstretched hand, in signs and wonders, and in His ordering of our lives. Without the power of God, our faith is baseless.

I came to know this truth through great trial. There was a time when a great confusion came over me and I wondered whether the power of God was real. I faced challenges to my untested faith. Deep, unanswerable questions plagued my mind. As the psalmist, "my feet had almost slipped; I had nearly lost my foothold" (Ps 73:2).

In life we will all face things that will test our faith. I encourage you today, do not doubt. When you feel weak before tough questions and mind-swirling issues, know that at this point God's power is being perfected in you. Decide to trust Him and rest in this.

God's power is real and if you just begin to walk in it you will never be the same again.

Be encouraged.

It's All About Jesus

He is before all things, and in him all things hold together. And he is the head of the body, the church; he is the beginning and the firstborn from among the dead, so that in everything he might have the supremacy. —Colossians 1:17-18

How wonderful it is to see the glory of Christ in all things. "The heavens declare the glory of God; the skies proclaim the work of his hands" (Ps 19:1). The Bible says the "rivers clap their hands and the mountains sing together for joy" (Ps. 98:8). Everything that is was made by him and bears the Master's quality and touch.

God made the things of the earth and called them good. Sin has skewed them, but they still bear surpassing beauty for those who would take the time to look and see. It is time to understand that when we worship, we only join in what all else in Creation already does.

A man of God once saw this truth and wondered. In a moment of revelation Charles Finney of the great 19th Century American revivals saw how every created thing—the trees, the grass, animals, and all—gave God glory. He wept at the fact that, of all things living, humanity alone denied Him worship.

May we all have this revelation and be encouraged by Creation around us to worship Him in the beauty of holiness.

A Blessing

The Lord was with Joseph and he pros-
pered, and he lived in the house of his
Egyptian master. —Genesis 39:2

The Lord is with you to prosper you. It is His loving desire to bless you in whatever you set your
hands to do. He wants for you to be blessed so that
you can be a blessing.

You should consistently see God's blessings in
your life. Even in hard and undesirable situations,
you should experience His favor. Unfortunately, too
many cannot boast in Him in this way. They live
their lives on the borders of His blessings, never div-
ing in.

This should not be for you. Let today be your day
to test the waters of God's grace. He wants to bless
you, not for you to waste it on your lusts, but for you
to be a blessing. You cannot truly be a blessing without His strength. Step out and be encouraged.

Nothing But Jesus

I have been crucified with Christ and I no longer live, but Christ lives in me. The life I live in the body, I live by faith in the Son of God, who loved me and gave himself for me. —Galatians 2:20

Are you identified with Christ? Often we attempt to live the Christian life by trying to imitate Christ. We tell God, "I will do my best." Our efforts to act like Christ do not please God however. He is only pleased when we give up rights to ourselves and are crucified with Christ.

When we are crucified with Christ, we consistently tell God, "It does not matter what pleases me, only what pleases you." When we identify with Christ, we are willing to give up having some things that are good to us—even when nothing is really wrong with them in themselves. We do not want anything to distract us from Jesus. All we really want is Him.

When we get this priority in our lives, we will have the motivation to go the extra mile to get off the defensive court of life. Lesser things will not sway us. Jesus becomes an anchor for us. When we have the urge to go overboard, our focus on Jesus reminds us of what is really important and what our standard of life is. We cannot fool ourselves into investing in what is good over what is better. When we identify with him, Christ begins to live in and through us. We are no longer just trying to imitate him.

Want nothing but Jesus. Know that there is no better thing. Give yourself wholly to him today and the Holy Spirit will take over.

Pray Continually

Pray continually. —1 Thessalonians 5:17

Your prayer life is your spiritual life. You have no true walk with God without consistent prayer. God is in your life. The scriptures advise, "If we live by the Spirit, we should walk in the Spirit." You should experience what you have.

There are two "secrets" to having a powerful prayer life. Know to whom you are praying. Study the Scriptures and understand who God is. Seek to understand His character and the power of His person. God is not our childhood friend, but He is our heavenly Father. Approach Him with reverential fear and fondness as from a child's heart.

The other "secret" is to understand timing. There should be a time set aside to put all else aside so that you can focus on the Lord. Both schedule times for prayer and learn to pray believing prayers throughout the day.

When you pray, believe you will receive. Do not pray and then take on the burden of answering the prayer yourself. Learn to pray with a sense of giving yourself over to God for Him to take care of you.

Remember what Jesus said, "The work of God is to believe on me" (John 6:29). We practice the work of believing by praying always, both in scheduled times and intermittently throughout the day. Take this, and be encouraged.

Waste Yourself

When the disciples saw this, they were indignant. "Why this waste?" they asked.
—Matthew 26:8

Do you waste yourself on Jesus? Jesus is so wonderfully impressed with those that do not mind wasting themselves on him.

In the scenario of the above Scripture, a relatively poor young woman takes an expensive alabaster box filled with a rich perfume and indiscriminately pours it out on Jesus. The box and its contents were worth almost a year's wages. When the disciples saw what was done, the Scriptures say, "they were indignant." They could have sold and used this valuable treasure for the poor, they said. But, Jesus disagreed. He took pleasure in what the young woman did.

In our service to the Lord, never feel like waste is wrong. Does God have you in a place where you feel like you are wasting your time or talents? Do you feel like you could be doing better somewhere else, if only the Lord would release you from your assignment? Maybe if you gave a little here and then spend yourself on things you consider more worthwhile? You may do well, but you would never find contentment or fulfillment.

No one is fulfilled simply accomplishing tasks for the Lord; we are fulfilled only in wasting ourselves. Because when we waste ourselves, our goal is not

the work, it is the pleasure of the Lord.
    Be encouraged.

We Are Winners

I can do everything through him who gives me strength. —Philippians 4:13

These words are both inspirational and powerful. Paul explains in the verses preceding that he had learned "in whatever state I am to be content." The lesson we can learn from God is how not to be tossed around in the roller coaster of life. We are winners and we must learn to behave like winners.

This is a blessed revelation. It shows us that even in spite of ourselves we may overcome problems. It gives us motivation to persist. When things do not go well, we may know that they will "turn out." By His grace, we are winners.

Be diligent and strive for excellence. Do your best and be confident. God is with you and will cause you to win every time.

Be a winner and be encouraged!

Changing Circumstances

On the day the Lord gave the Amorites over to Israel, Joshua said to the Lord in the presence of Israel: "O sun, stand still over Gibeon, O moon, over the Valley of Aijalon." —Joshua 10:12

Some of us feel trapped. We are displeased by commitments we have made. We feel trapped by our jobs, our relationships, our finances, maybe even our church. Past mistakes have ensnared us and present problems make things worse. We do not have to handle these things in our own strength. We can change our circumstances with the power of God.

I recently read an article verifying the Bible's testimony that God sent a massive flood on the earth. Late studies have shown the fall of Jericho happened as remarkably as the Scriptures say. When God moves, the changes in His wake are measurable and can be quantified.

Do not think all God can do is give us hope and a good feeling. God has power to change things. Many confess this, but few lean on this truth. Do not feel trapped, beloved. When God is ready for you to move, nothing can hold you back.

Be your best in the place that you are. The circumstances will change when you learn how to trust God where you are. Be encouraged.

Intercession

Then the king said to the man of God, "Intercede with the Lord your God and pray for me that my hand may be restored." So the man of God interceded with the Lord, and the king's hand was restored and became as it was before.
—1 Kings 13:6

We release God grace and power through the ministry of intercession. Sometimes we wonder, "Does prayer change things, or does it just change me?" It does both. God affects great and mighty things in and through us by prayer.

God waits on our prayers. He has placed this great responsibility in our hands. Do not be discouraged should your prayers seem to go unanswered. Know that God is answering. Sometimes He must work something quietly in you before He does something for you. The appearance of unanswered prayer is disheartening. You must hold firmly to the truth that God answers all prayers.

Pray, therefore, with faith. Do not lose hope when you pray because things to do not happen right away. Your prayers, by God's grace, move heaven and earth to accomplish His meaningful desires. Pray with diligence and fervor, believing you have received that for which you believed. It will be done.

Be encouraged.

What it Takes

When Jacob awoke from his sleep, he thought, "Surely the Lord is in this place, and I was not aware of it." —Genesis 28:16

The Christian life is a process of growth and maturity. God calls us to maturity in the body of Christ. We never stop growing, but there is a level of maturity we can reach where we live full of faith and of the Spirit.

We begin our journey by being able to see things from a spiritual perspective and learning to see God's hand in situations. God is at work around you, whether you recognize it or not. The spiritual walk begins when you pay attention, take the time to see what He is doing, and join Him.

This is what it takes to live the Christian life. Some people reduce the Christian life to "moral living" or going to church. Others believe it is "knowing your Bible" and confessing doctrines. All these things are important, but the key to the Christian life is walking with God. And to walk with Him, we must see Him in our lives.

Be encouraged.

See What God Has Done

. . . It will now be said of Jacob and of Israel, 'See what God has done!'
—Numbers 23:23

It is important that we learn to see what God has done in our lives. Without this knowledge, our Christian life becomes powerless and our vigor turns to listlessness. Walking with Christ depends on our ability to see what God is doing in and around us. Seeing is the gateway into spiritual maturity.

How do we see? The way in which we see is through trusting. "Trust in the LORD with all your heart and lean not on your own understanding; in all your ways acknowledge him, and he will make your paths straight" (Prov. 3:5-6). We trust the Lord through observing the principles of His Word and expecting His results. We see through rightly adjusting our behavior to fit God's precepts and commands. When we follow God's Word, we will see God's will.

Be careful of ritualistic observance of God's Word. We do not behave righteously to gain "brownie points" with God. Righteousness is the gateway to revelation. Let us go through the gate and be encouraged.

A Life of Love

...live a life of love, just as Christ loved us and gave himself up for us as a fragrant offering and sacrifice to God. —Ephesians 5:2

The second step toward spiritual maturity is self-sacrificial love. We must first see God at work around us and cease our own works to labor in Him. (Heb. 4:10-11) This is called a labor of love.

I have at times lamentably become so "spiritually deep" that I missed the most important things. God wants us to commit to a life of love. Plain and simple.

Judge all your words, thoughts and actions on this principle. Let God's love envelope your heart and set yourself to pour it out to others continuously. Think about all those who really seem to represent Christ. They pour out love.

May this reminder be a blessing to you. Be encouraged.

Loving Fear

...what does the Lord your God ask of you but to fear the Lord your God, to walk in all his ways, to love him, to serve the Lord your God with all your heart and with all your soul. —Deuteronomy 10:12

The fear of the Lord is essential to our assurance of salvation and growth in Christ. We will not rightly abide in Him, unless we understand the consequence of not abiding. Though He "works in us to will and do His good pleasure," He daily gives us the joy of choosing Him. Not only must we be inclined toward God, we must continue in Him by the free choice of our will.

We may be assured that by the regeneration of our hearts, that we will always be moved to choose rightly. If our faith at the point of our salvation was true, it is durative—saving faith remains. Yet, this does not negate the clear need for the Scriptures to admonish us to remain in Christ. Part of God's process in securing us is warning us of not abiding in the Lord.

One may ask, "What if we one day do not choose to abide? What if we sin?" These two questions are very different. Should we sin, we have an advocate with the Father. As we abide in Christ, he will divinely restore us to right fellowship. If after knowing the truth about God, we turn from Him, we were never changed in the first place. Otherwise, our hearts would irrevocably call out for Him.

"Therefore . . . be all the more eager to make your calling and election sure. For if you do these things, you will never fall" (2 Pet 1:10). Choose to abide in Him and serve Him today, so that your fruit will testify to you daily of the eternal security God has provided for you. Be encouraged.

Set to Serve

It is the Lord your God you must follow, and him you must revere. Keep his commands and obey him; serve him and hold fast to him. —Deuteronomy 13:4

We must be set to serve. It is not an automatic process or inclination. Though we may love to serve, it is our responsibility to see that our hearts are continually prepared for it.

Have you ever gotten on a roll, doing what you know you should, only to fall off track? When things have gone well, I have even wondered at times how long it would last.

The fact is, we must be set to serve. It is work and not something we can do "on autopilot." We must set ourselves to make good choices about our time, our energy and our motivation. We must use wisdom and properly invest our limited resources. We must set ourselves to do without sometimes and enjoy the dignity of budgeting what we have.

We must resist splurging and baseless spending. We must cultivate a hatred of the evil of a life not submitted to purpose. When we sin, we must confess the whole sin—not just what we have done, but why we did it. And we must not confess simply to avert a sense of guilt; we must confess with an urgency to get things right.

Set yourself to serve the Lord. Revere Him, hold

fast to Him, remember His holiness. Stay close to Him and meditate on His Word. Do not be superficial, but serve Him with all your heart. If we do this, we will see great fruit consistently produced in our lives.

From Faith to Faith

If I have the gift of prophecy and can fathom all mysteries and all knowledge, and if I have a faith that can move mountains, but have not love, I am nothing.
—1 Corinthians 13:2

The beginning and end of the Christian life is love. It is the foundation upon which we grow and it is as well the goal of our maturity. When we lay our lives on the altar of love, we can grow from faith to faith.

The Bible teaches, "Knowledge puffs up, but love builds up" (1 Cor. 8:1b). Love must guide our growth. It is not enough to know the Word, to be in a leadership position, or to train in ministry. We must build our ministry skills, but this should only be because of our love for God and for others. "The only thing that counts is faith expressing itself through love" (Gal 5:6b).

I encourage you today to remember love as a motivation and a goal. A real Christian is a man or woman of love. Commit to a growth where love is the key and be encouraged.

Christ Depends on It

"Why are you sleeping?" he asked them.
"Get up and pray so that you will not fall
into temptation." —Luke 22:46

Why would God, who has all power, need us? Does Christ, who has "all authority in heaven and earth," depend on us? The answer is, "Yes."

The Bible says that Christ dwells in our hearts by faith. (Eph. 3:17) The night before his crucifixion, Messiah prayed that we would all be one "to let the world know that you sent me and have loved them even as you have loved me." (John 17:23) The condition upon which Christ is greatly manifested in the earth depends on what we do.

Surely, God is still in control. He "works in us to will and do His good pleasure" (Phil. 2:13). He who "began a good work in you will carry it on to completion until the day of Christ Jesus" (Phil. 1:6). Yet, He waits on us to respond out of free will and in faithful obedience to His will and pleasure.

Therefore, let us come together as the body of Christ like never before. Pray diligently and at every opportunity for the saints and for the world. Earnestly share the love of Christ with hurting people everywhere. Intercede and support missions around the world.

Let us "step up to the plate," for Christ depends on it. Be encouraged.

Keeping It Real

The Lord turned and looked straight at Peter. Then Peter remembered the word the Lord had spoken to him: "Before the rooster crows today, you will disown me three times." —Luke 22:61

Keep it real, beloved. There is no room for phoney-ness in Christ. Stop making promises you will not keep. Stop swearing against your own honor the changes you will make in your life. Stop making oaths in the Name of God that you cannot keep. Stop pretending everything with you is always so wonderful. Be real.

When we are real, we can get the help we need. God has provided us help and strength to continuously have victory in our lives. But, this victory is dependent on our humility and meekness (vulnerability). (Ps. 18:27; 37:11; Matt. 5:5)

We often feel the pressure to be a "super-saint." This just will not do! We serve a "super-Savior" who "works in us to will and do His good pleasure" (Phil. 2:13). When God works in us, He expects us to submit to the process. He expects us to be real about who we are with Him. When we are, He will take us to new and greater heights.

I encourage you today, my friends, to learn how to admit when you are wrong. Say, "I'm sorry" often. Laugh at yourself at times. Confess your sins to God for His forgiveness and forgive yourselves. Be real, beloved, plain and simple.

The Fellowship

You will be betrayed even by parents, brothers, relatives and friends, and they will put some of you to death. —Luke 21:16

Betrayal is a monstrous cut to the human heart. God has made our hearts to relate to others. He did not create us to stand alone and made clear the vice of it early on. (Gen. 2:18) However we may try to deny it, we were made to fellowship with others.

Fellowship involves trust and dependence. Often I have heard, "I don't trust in any man, only God alone!" How I cringe at such words. Scripture guides us away from basing our lives on others. Yet, we are also called to a love that "always trusts" (1 Cor. 13:7).

We must learn the real power of real fellowship. We must be able to tell the difference between real and superficial heart connections, for the days to come are evil.

Be encouraged.

Do What You Are Supposed to Do

Moses said to the Lord, "You have been telling me, 'Lead these people,' but you have not let me know whom you will send with me. You have said, 'I know you by name and you have found favor with me.' If you are pleased with me, teach me your ways so I may know you and continue to find favor with you. Remember that this nation is your people." —Exodus 33:12-13

Dear friends, it is incumbent on us to do what God has assigned us to do. The Bible teaches us not to "think of yourself more highly than you ought, but rather think of yourself with sober judgment, in accordance with the measure of faith God has given you" (Rom. 12:3). We should not think more highly of ourselves than we ought, but we, with "sober judgment" should not abdicate our responsibility either.

You are who you are. If you are a father, lead your household. If you are a mother, be strong for your family. Discipline your children and bring order to your house. Do your job and stop trying to do others. Find your place. Define it well. With gentleness and love, keep your task before you and do not get side-tracked.

If you have authority, use it. Be meek, but not weak. Walk in the strength of the Lord. Stand up for what is right and do it. Stop compromising your witness by a lack of diligence and consistency. Strengthen yourself and build your skills. Ask questions and seek answers. Stop settling for less and assuming things just cannot be done. Where there is God, there is always a way. Necessity is the mother of invention—stop giving up when things seem difficult or complex.

Do what you are supposed to do, beloved, be encouraged.

Breaking Spiritual Barriers

Then Jesus was led by the Spirit into the desert to be tempted by the devil.
—Matthew 4:1

What do you do when the devil offers you the world? This question is pivotal to the process of spiritual growth. Know that at every level of growth in the Spirit, Satan will tempt you with a counterfeit.

Too many of us are waylaid in our walk with God, falling for Satan's deceptions. He tempted Jesus with bread; he may tempt us with sleep or relationships or money or position. These things are generally good and Satan's trick is for us to choose the good over God.

Satan does not start by tempting us with terrible things. He uses good things playing on our conviction that God has good things for us. The issue is that every good thing we have should come from God through godly process.

Be careful of quick fixes and "success-come-easy." When God gives us something, He gives it to make us love the Giver above the gift. Be encouraged.

Let's Get to It

But when Amasa went to summon Judah, he took longer than the time the king had set for him. —2 Samuel 20:5

Procrastination is the key to certain failure. It is the opposite of the diligence that God blesses with success. I have seen clearly that God's blessing is strong on the steadfast hand. Though He meets us in our shortcomings, God is not likely to strengthen an undermined mind.

Our task is to pour ourselves into the important things, not just the urgent. Rebuke the mindset trapped in a crisis mentality. Though crises give us energy and help our motivation, they often leave us spent with very little fruit to show for it. Remember in particular the little things that are important. Organize yourself around them and make it a challenge in completing them.

It is time for many of us to take charge of our lives again. Overwhelming to-do lists of things conquers our lives. We must rid ourselves of this unrighteous occupation. The Bible teaches us to "repent of dead works" (Heb. 6:1, KJV). Let us be obedient for Christ's sake and for ours. Be encouraged.

Let's Get Out There

When David was told, "Look, the Philistines are fighting against Keilah and are looting the threshing floors," he inquired of the Lord, saying, "Shall I go and attack these Philistines?" The Lord answered him, "Go, attack the Philistines and save Keilah." —1 Samuel 23:1-2

David was inspired by a strength greater than his. He worked great things through that strength. His successes and triumphs were not based on charisma, ability, skill, style or strength. He excelled in life due to his reliance on God's strength.

Too many of us never try God. We should not test Him with foolishness yet He does call us to try Him. He wants to astonish us with the works of His arm. We often quaver before the opportunities God gives us, yet He still beckons us to "try Me."

If we would fulfill our purpose in life, we must get out of our resting places. We must get out into the world. God is calling us. Many need to be saved, and though we have not the strength ourselves, we must go in Jesus Name!

I encourage you today to go.

Difference from You

If then I do not grasp the meaning of what someone is saying, I am a foreigner to the speaker, and he is a foreigner to me.
—1 Corinthians 14:11

Many people live lives radically different from ours. They have their own idioms and standards. They dress differently and we have trouble pronouncing their names. They speak different languages and eat "strange" foods. What will you say about those that are different from you?

Christ charges us to be humble and loving. We must not quickly judge when people are different from us. They may come from a culture or country we despise. They may smell differently. Nevertheless, we are to love them and to know them.

Our task as Christians is to love others with Christ's love. If we are to love someone, we must get to know them. In this time of fear and mistrust, let us take the lead in reaching out, sharing and loving. Many are different from you, but they need Jesus just the same.

Be encouraged.

The Importance of Change

God, who is enthroned forever, will hear them and afflict them men who never change their ways and have no fear of God. —Psalm 55:19

Our God is awesome! He never changes, yet He proceeds from one point to another in the progression of His will! It is a fallacy to think that God, like us, resists change and fears it. He is stable in who He is and can handle change.

Though God never changes or flutters in His thinking, He clearly causes change in the earth. Once we sacrificed through the blood of animals, now we depend on the blood of the Lamb. Once we served Him through circumcision and observations, now we see Him without these veils. Once we knew Him through a book only, now we know Him by His Spirit through power and suffering. (Phil. 3:10) Change is important, because it is the power of maturity and the fulfillment of purpose.

Why do we fear change? Typically, it is because we are not stable. God shows us to be. Find your peace not in a structure or a creed or a routine. Find your peace in a dynamic relationship with God. For without change we will perish like fools.

Be encouraged.

Stick to the Basics

*Watch your life and doctrine closely.
Persevere in them, because if you do, you
will save both yourself and your hearers.
—1 Timothy 4:16*

Sometimes in the rush to achieve spiritual maturity, we often forget the basics. One can perceive deep things and understand many issues, only to be defeated because one's prayer life was not in order. God is not interested in charisma, but character. As we seek to grow in Christ, let us not forget the basics.

Basic Christianity deals with the little things we must do to hold an enriching relationship with God and people. It involves prayer, meditation on God's Word, sharing, serving, learning, obeying, confessing, repenting, and witnessing, witnessing, witnessing. I would suppose all who hold to the faith do these things. Yet, doing them with a rhythm and balance is important.

How is your love life with the Lord? What is the degree of your devotion? What time are you giving to your relationship with Him? When you witness, can you get straight to the point or do you always seem to get deep with no fruitful results?

Stick to the basics, beloved. Keep a good order in your life and be encouraged.

The Kingdom Has Come

But if I drive out demons by the Spirit of God, then the kingdom of God has come upon you. —Matthew 12:28

Do not be so focused on the future that you do not see the power of the moment. It is entirely possible that some of our ineffectiveness in the Body of Christ lies in our propensity to put people in a time machine. Either we are pushing them back, reliving past glories, or we are pushing forward in time to some ethereal hope in the future. We as Christians must learn the power of now.

Purpose in the past and the significance of the future bears upon the present. We should not discount the usefulness of studying what has gone before or planning for what is to come. Yet, let us not get stuck with our heart and emotions tied in either. Many of us base our faith and hope on what God has done before or what He is getting ready to do.

This temporal schizophrenia makes us ineffective for the moment. By it we wait for God's kingdom to come, when He will set things aright and fix all problems. Yet, the kingdom has come in the sense of God's Spirit reaching the world through us, the Body of Christ!

People have very present problems need us present with them. Dream big, consider your ways, but, by all means, seize the moment!

Infidelity

Good understanding wins favor, but the way of the unfaithful is hard. —Proverbs 13:15

What do you do when everything of true value is lost in a moment? Too many souls are mortally wounded by infidelity. Too many families have been split down the middle. There are too many vendettas and dreams of revenge snatching hearts from sensible thought. The way of the unfaithful is truly hard.

What balm or healing cream can soothe the burn of infidelity's scorch? Can God's grace truly apply when we really, really do not deserve it?

My heart pities those who continually make wrong choices. It is such a quandary to know that a "changing grace" is available by faith, yet so many have not claimed it. Their way is hard and their judgment will be just, but it does not have to be that way for them.

All of us deal with unfaithfulness in one way or another. It is either to God, a spouse, a friend, a job or whatever. The shame is stifling and the bondage very real. But, my friend, the Bible says, "But where sin increased, grace increased all the more" (Rom. 5:20).

Consider this and be encouraged.

Real Wealth

I know your afflictions and your poverty—
yet you are rich! I know the slander of
those who say they are Jews and are not,
but are a synagogue of Satan.
—Revelation 2:9

I once shared in a mission trip to Uganda. This beautiful country rests in central Africa, on the northern edge of Lake Victoria from which the River Nile extends. Once called the "pearl of Africa" by Sir. Winston Churchill, the nation won its independence from British rule in 1962. Various ethnic struggles from within and without and the dictatorships that followed have however left the country economically depleted.

Our team served with a local pastor in a regional conference of churches. Men and women of churches and ministries from Uganda, Rwanda, Congo and other surrounding nations were present. This young pastor was a tremendous leader with a church of more than three thousand members. He had established well over one hundred churches in several African nations. It was by his vision and great faith that hundreds of church leaders gathered all day for eight days for teaching, impartation and encouragement.

I came from America with my colleagues to impart. Yet, I often felt dwarfed by the largeness and efficiency of that ministry for the sake of the Kingdom. We consider ourselves so rich in the West and lean so heavily on our wealth to get things done for the kingdom. But, they displayed real wealth in Uganda. There I saw a wealth in relationships, in character and in purpose. I saw a wealth in utility as they made use of everything. Nothing was wasted on frivolity. In Uganda, we felt like royalty, not because of rich and lavish outpourings of material things, but of sincere love and affection.

The Bible speaks of the Smyrnian church in Revelation as poor—yet, they had true wealth. I have certainly seen an example of this in modern times and I bless God for seeing it.

May this recollection be an encouragement to you today.

Save Us Again

My dear children, for whom I am again in the pains of childbirth until Christ is formed in you. —Galatians 4:19

What we know is that Christ died once for the sins of all. By this, God has made available His grace to a dying world and saves us once and for all in Christ. This being said, we must also recognize a sense in which we are saved day by day.

Trying to avoid spurious doctrine, we often limit the word salvation to our eternal destiny. Yet, this is not so in the Bible. Actually, salvation in the Bible speaks to health and wholeness. Biblically speaking, we are brought to wholeness on a daily basis.

The fact of our daily "salvation" is good news. Yesterday's sins, weakness and mistakes do not control our todays and tomorrows. New morning mercies wrest from them their otherwise deadly potency. The good news of the gospel is that we can get back up again and keep getting back up.

Do not knock the process through which God is growing you. It may look ugly, haphazard and clumsy, but God is really dealing with us with a profound grace. May the entire church of Christ be encouraged with this message and cry out in fervor, "Lord, save us again!"

And What Shall We Do?

Now there were four men with leprosy at the entrance of the city gate. They said to each other, "Why stay here until we die?
—2 Kings 7:3

The opportunity to reach the world is before us. What shall we do with it? Shall we stay safely within our churches and denominational structures? Shall we wait in the stalls and not charge? Shall we sacrifice the great commission to maintain the little we have already possessed?

The harvest depends on those who no longer have anything to lose. It belongs to those that will no longer sit, waiting to die. If we do not bless the world and reach out, we will miss our assignment. Our time on earth will be spent simply waiting to get to heaven. This will not please God when we see Him.

What shall we do? Let us set our hearts to go beyond the borders and to reach the nations. We must raise a movement in this generation that will not die out when we die. Be courageous, knowing the Great Work depends on us.

Delight

Delight yourself in the Lord and he will give you the desires of your heart. —Psalm 37:4

We ought not to trust in our own strength. Though He may have given us much of it, God yet wants us to depend on Him. "Commit your way to the LORD; trust in him . . . " is what the Word says. (Ps. 37:5) This calls us to have faith God who is "able to do exceeding abundantly above what we can ask or think."

When we delight ourselves in God, we rejoice in His faithfulness and marvel at His grace toward us. Scripture calls us to delight in the Lord instead of our own strength so that we might see His wondrous work on our behalf. Another way to put this admonition is: "Delight to see what God will do if you only trust Him."

What a way to live our lives! We may not only see miracles, but to expect them! How wonderful it is to see God's hand working for us in definite ways. It is truly a delight to know He loves us and to see Him show it day after day. Know this delight today and be encouraged.

A Whole New World

Since, then, you have been raised with Christ, set your hearts on things above, where Christ is seated at the right hand of God. —Col 3:1

As Christians, we are bound to a whole new world. It is true that we are in the world, but we are not of it and we must tread carefully. It is easy to become wrapped again in this world's allurements. The Bible warns us that if we "have escaped the corruption of the world by knowing our Lord and Savior Jesus Christ and are again entangled in it and overcome, [we] are worse off at the end than [we] were at the beginning" (2 Pet. 2:20)

If we will escape the lure of the world's pleasures, we must know the true and everlasting pleasures in Christ. And if we are to know what Christ offers, we must study and seek to know. What does this mean? We must learn of the whole new world to which we are bound and discover how to enjoy its bounty.

We must stop living as if this world were all there is and take to ourselves the precious promises God has laid up for us in His Word. Change your perspective. Make your mind up to enjoy what comes from and flows to the Kingdom. Do not take a break from focusing on things above—where Christ is. Let your heart and hope be enraptured by a whole new world.

Be encouraged.

Learn

It was good for me to be afflicted so that I might learn your decrees. —Psalm 119:71

There is a difference between learning and understanding. We grasp truth through understanding, but learning changes our behavior. When it comes to God's Word we must learn and not simply understand.

Learning requires a deeper, more intricate processes than understanding. Learning comes through experiencing and overcoming a challenge or crisis and requires faith and commitment. When faith and commitment are missing, we may know what is right, but find ourselves frustrated in our attempts to do it consistently.

God uses the challenges that we face in this sinful world to teach us. He does not send trials our way for this reason. But, sometimes He might. Whatever the case, God uses our crises to bring us up to another level. If we apply ourselves to learning, we will overcome the challenge successfully—God will see to this. If we do not, the challenge will come again, maybe in a different form or intensity.

Let us understand that the trials we face cannot destroy us because of the grace that works within us. But, we can miss our lessons and find ourselves embittered and embattled. Know that what you are facing will make you stronger if you set your heart to learning from it.

Be encouraged.

Listen

Listen and hear my voice; pay attention and hear what I say. —Isaiah 28:23

We must be careful to give attention to the voice of the Lord. The Bible says that "man does not live by bread alone." We live by "every word proceeding out of the mouth of God." God is speaking or has spoken to us, and if we would live victoriously in Christ, we must listen.

Listening requires humility and a resistance to offence. We will not always like what we hear. It may not always "feel" true. But, to listen properly, we must be patient and not reactive. God has some things to say to us that will help us, though it may be like bad-tasting medicine.

Let us hear what God has to say to us through His Word, the Bible, through prayer and through godly counsel. God's words may come during your devotion time or through a Sunday service message. God may be speaking to you through a mature Christian friend or the still small voice of His Spirit. I say to you today, let us not harden our hearts. Let us listen and be encouraged.

Eternal Life

Now this is eternal life: that they may know you, the only true God, and Jesus Christ, whom you have sent. —John 17:3

Eternal life is so much more than living forever. It is an abundant life. (John 10:10) Someone once stated: "God's blessings are better in a better way." This is a very rich statement.

God can do "exceeding and abundantly more than we ask or think" (Eph. 3:20). His blessings and gifts of grace to us are always better than what we could do on our own. Yet, they are also better in a better way. God blesses us with what really matters. He does not just us with stuff. God gives us things to make us better.

Eternal life is not simply about longevity. It enhances every moment with the knowledge that God is with us and will be with us forever. The blessing and essence of eternal life is our relationship with Him.

May the Lord encourage you today.

Dependability

It does not, therefore, depend on man's desire or effort, but on God's mercy.
—Romans 9:16

Many of us at one time or another have been hurt by someone's lack of dependability. This pushes us to be cynical, angry and confused. Even when we ourselves can improve in our faithfulness to others, it is discouraging to experience the unfaithfulness of others that we have trusted.

How should we respond when others let us down? We must first remember ourselves and be humble. Psalms says, "The LORD preserves the faithful, but the proud he pays back in full" (Ps. 31:23). If we surrender our injury to God, He will preserve us and work things out in time.

Once we have humbled ourselves, we can speak honestly. Honest words from a humble heart are powerful and effective. They are like seeds sown in good soil. They will bring back a good harvest.

I have both afflicted and been afflicted with a lack of dependability. As for the former, I have learned that an honest apology and true concern for others helps. We must learn how to set limits and be faithful to our time and commitments. When we are not, we must be true to our commitments and accountable when we have not fulfilled them. Receive this and be encouraged.

Winning When We Lose

We are hard pressed on every side, but not crushed; perplexed, but not in despair; persecuted, but not abandoned; struck down, but not destroyed. —2 Corinthians 4:8-9

We will all lose sometimes. Losing is a part of life. It is when we lose that thinking ourselves winners becomes most difficult.

Learn how to enjoy losing. God will teach you how to win when you lose. You must exercise true faith. Faith is not an unfounded hope or blind confidence. Faith is upholding the truth of God's Word against all odds. By faith we may watch God make something out of nothing.

As a child of God, you are a winner by default. When discouraging situations come, learn to trust in God's love for you. Lean on the fact that in the end you will be on top. Learn from your failures and, when necessary, to make things right with others involved.

Take confidence in the Lord and His plan for your life. The only thing that will kill your destiny is quitting. With this confidence in your heart, humble yourself and learn to walk in things God has for you.

Be encouraged.

Being Encouraged

Rejoice in the Lord always. I will say it again: Rejoice! —Philippians 4:4

Rejoicing is an intentional process taken to witness to the truth. It is not always automatic or in response to something. We must learn to walk in an attitude of rejoicing at all times.

Sometimes we separate in our minds practical truth and the idea of truth. Therefore, we can know with our minds that we have victory in Jesus, but not trust our heart to this. The true test of whether we believe something is whether or not we are willing to wager our lives on it.

Our victory in Jesus is a practical truth. No matter what you are going through, you are going to win in the end as a child of God. The choice is whether we are going to enjoy the process or not. Be encouraged today. Keep your head up and rejoice. The Lord will never abandon you, nor will He leave you alone.

What Now?

For this very reason, make every effort to add to your faith goodness; and to goodness, knowledge; and to knowledge, self-control; and to self-control, perseverance; and to perseverance, godliness; and to godliness, brotherly kindness; and to brotherly kindness, love. —2 Peter 1:5-7

Maturity in our walk with God is a never-ending process. It involves the development of many different kinds of virtue. Yet, often, when we seem to master one type or another, we find ourselves asking the question, "What next?"

We must avoid this deception from the enemy. We never arrive in Christ, we only continue to press. We should base our sense of effectiveness not on our apparent successes (i.e., souls saved, changed habits, successful ministry), but on our perpetual sense of pressing. We must always keep faith and integrity in our walk with God.

One of my personal heroes affirmed this once. Watchman Nee was invited to London and America by a certain group of Christians. His hosts possessed a smugness about their understanding of the faith. They would state, "What manner of knowledge or revelation do we not have?" Watchman, very perturbed by this saying, arose at the end of his time with them and said, "My brothers, your knowledge of the Scriptures and doctrine is very broad and vast. But, it would mean only this much in China," and he snapped his fingers definitively, "if you could not cast one demon out."

There is always so much more to learn. Think of this not as a burden, but as a great joy. For the Lord is vast and mighty and we have not moved one inch into understanding His true glory.

Be encouraged.

Little Faith?

He replied, "Because you have so little faith. I tell you the truth, if you have faith as small as a mustard seed, you can say to this mountain, 'Move from here to there' and it will move. Nothing will be impossible for you." —Matthew 17:20

"When the Son of Man comes, will he find faith on the earth" (Luke 18:8)? What a profound question. This generation suffers from a lack of faith. Not only is there lack, there is confusion.

What is faith? There is a philosophical definition and a practical one. We know it is the "substance of things hoped for, evidence of things not seen," but practically it is believing that God is and that He is a rewarder of those that actively and consistently seek Him. (Heb. 11:1,6) Faith is the assuredness in God to press into His presence, never to be denied our godly request.

We need not lack this assurance. It is true, some things for which we prayed that did not happen. Do not let that stop you or plant in your heart seeds of doubt. Press in His presence even more and learn of Him. In the end, God will answer and make you greater.

Seek God when you pray and not just answers. Do not be discouraged when God does not deliver what you order. You do not need the "things," you need God. His grace is always sufficient.

Be encouraged.

Finding Faith

". . . when the Son of Man comes, will he find faith on the earth?" —Luke 18:8

Faith involves persistence. It is the anchor of determination. We show it through what we do. When we approach God, God is pleased to see our faith in the manner and diligence with which we approach Him. The faith God honors is a steadfast, powerful faith. This is the faith we need to see more of today.

Statistics suggests, if the trend continues, that only 4% of this new generation will confess Christ in their adult ages. That compares with 25% of the baby boomer generation and 67% of the Post WWII generation. This is a tragedy, yet a great opportunity.

In the darkness, the light shines brighter. People need to see true faith. They need to see a real and dynamic relationship with the Father. Jesus fretted in his day about how faith in the Father had become superficial. He asked the question: "When the Son of man returns, will there be faith on the earth?" It is time we get "sold out" and explode in this generation for Christ. Be encouraged.

Discernment and Correction

. . . rebuke a discerning man, and he will gain knowledge. —Proverbs 19:25

One of the greatest challenges for the church today is knowing and doing the will of God. As unbelievable as it may sound, many do not believe we can discover God's will in particular. This is a disease in the church that comes from its going to bed with the world. We have become a church without discernment.

Discernment is the major function of wisdom. A discerning man is a wise man. It is the ability to look into the issues of life and to perceive God's will and God's way. A "sold out" Christian is one that is only interested in God's perspective.

There are many set ways to gain God's perspective. One of the most important ways is through correction. God uses our failures to teach us. We all mess up, lose, do wrong things and give wrong responses. Often our natural response is to rear up with pride when we face correction for our wrongdoing. This is very foolish. When someone rebukes us, no matter how or by who, we should learn to learn from the correction.

Receiving a rebuke is a hard thing to do. It punctures our egos and we seem to lose face. I encourage you to think less of your ego and more about being God's child. This is where your true dignity is anyway.

Be encouraged.

The Normal Christian

"For who has known the mind of the Lord that he may instruct him?" But we have the mind of Christ. —1 Corinthians 2:16

So often we claim a victorious Christian life, but we do not live it. Those that walk closely with Christ and experience his victory over sin and the world, we see as super-Christians. They actually are not "super" at all. They are normal Christians.

What has become normal to us is actually spiritual malnutrition and anemia. There are certain people groups in the world that live with chronic sickness. One group actually bares a virus that causes blotches in their skin. These skin spots are normal for them— indeed, those without them are ostracized. The point is that they are used to being sick.

We too are used to being sick. But praise God for His tremendous love and care for His people. He is raising the standard, that His people may be well again! Do you not sense it? Can you feel it? God is burgeoning our spirits with this tremendous sense that there is more to life in Christ than what is considered "normal."

Jesus is saying to us, like to the man at the pool of Silaom, "Do you want to be made whole?" Do not sit idly at religious pools expecting one day something will happen. Do not be content with business as usual. Hear the Word from the Lord and be whole in God.

Be encouraged.

Avoiding Confusion

I am astonished that you are so quickly deserting the one who called you by the grace of Christ and are turning to a different gospel—which is really no gospel at all. Evidently some people are throwing you into confusion and are trying to pervert the gospel of Christ. —Galations 1:6-7

There is something called the gospel that in not the gospel at all. Beware of this. Jesus said, "you may tell a tree by its fruit." The fruit of the true gospel is reconciliation with God in love and holy fear. But, this other gospel produces nothing but confusion.

Let me ask: Can God create a rock that He cannot lift? Think about it. Can He who can do anything make something that He Himself cannot lift? What is the answer to this question? The answer is: this is a dumb question!

Some questions simply seek to produce deception. It seems to have legitimacy on the surface, but involves a contradiction in terms. It does not bring understanding and wisdom; it is sown full of deception and brings forth nothing but confusion.

Beloved avoid confusion at all costs! Press into His presence and do not seek after position, power or possession in this world. Clear your mind and spirit from the confusion of this "cultural Christianity" in which we live. God has so much more for those that seek Him with a pure heart. Be encouraged.

Wonderful Victory

No, in all these things we are more than conquerors through him who loved us.
—Romans 8:37

Victory is normal to the Christian life. As a child of God, we are "more than conquerors." Any notion to the contrary is a lie and is not the truth. By God's grace and the redeeming work of Christ, we stand above all else and cannot be dragged back.

Nothing can separate us from the love of Christ. Before you sinned, before you tripped and fell, before you made your last mistake, God knew you and sent His Son to die for you. God's love for you is not contingent upon what you do. It is pursuant and persistent. When you fall, learn a lesson as you sit there and, then, get back up and walk again. Turn off self-condemnation. The Bible says, when your heart condemns you, God is greater than your heart.

We have wonderful victory in Christ Jesus. He died to snatch us out of lonely darkness and to deliver us into the light of fellowship in the household of God. Do not consider that he will desert you. He will not. Therefore when doubt or fear attempts to set in, know we are more than conquerors over them all. Be encouraged.

One a Day

As you go, preach this message: 'The king-dom of heaven is near.' —Matthew 10:7

How's the work of God with you? There is a distinction between the church and the work of God. The church is the fellowship of believers where the work of God is done. The work is the mission of reaching and discipling souls for Christ. Often, we strengthen our churches, but forget the work.

How is the work of God with you? Are you a disciplemaker? Are you reproducing Christ in others? Beloved, going to church and "getting Word" just is not enough, is it? You have had a wonderful change in your life through growth in Christ, but something is missing, is it not?

Become a disciplemaker. Do the work of an evangelist. The Kingdom is near and the world needs to know! What if you witnessed to a different person every day for a year? Three hundred sixty five people for each day of the year. Do you think ten, maybe five, or one would become a disciple? How many disciples are you making now? Do you see it?

The mission of the Christ life has two prongs. We must live as Christ lived and we must witness to his saving power to the world. Two prongs. One without the other leads to failure. Try winning "one-a-day" and reach the world for Christ. Be encouraged.

Memorial Day

Remember the days of old; consider the generations long past. Ask your father and he will tell you, your elders, and they will explain to you. —Deuteronomy 32:7

Remembrance is an exercise underused in this generation. The Bible teaches us to consider our past and remember the generations that have gone before us. Yet, we often prance along into the future without the lessons of the past to guide us.

Our fast-paced society tempts us to simply "live for today." We lose sight of the sacrifices, triumphs, tragedies, and labors that enabled us to be where we are. Many of us refuse to look at the mistakes and sins of our own past, or the past generations of our family. But we must learn to see ourselves in context!

We flow in an ongoing river, from generation to generation. What we have, we received from those that have gone before. What our children will have, they will receive from us. Do not smile and coo at your baby now, if you do not intend to offer them a goodly heritage. Make up in your mind to see yourself in time, in this time, in our time. Remember the days of old and use that as a frame for your imagination. For, what will our children remember about us when we are gone?

Be encouraged.

Sudan

Remember my chains. —Colossians 4:18

I once went to Rome and sat in a little underground cell used in ancient times as a jail. The small compartment was accessible by stairway when I was there, but in ancient times, only through a hole about three feet in diameter. It would have been dark, damp and dirty, filled with rodents, and filth. They say that very cell was where Paul was chained for his testimony of faith.

There is tremendous persecution of Christians across the globe, including China, Indonesia, Vietnam, Sri Lanka, India and other parts. But, I want to highlight Sudan for now as a representative case to show how bad things are in this new millennium. In Sudan there is slavery, forced famine, physical torture and efforts at genocide upon the largely Black and Christian south.

Christians still die for the Gospel. Persecution is real. We have misappropriated the term here in the States and maybe in other nations. We dramatize our colds and personal problems as persecution—but it is not. Persecution is the suffering that comes because of a stand for the truth. It is represented in torture and inflicted pain and death. We should not trivialize it—Christians still die.

Let us pray for our brethren in Sudan and around the world and remember them who are in chains for the Gospel. Be encouraged.

Victory and Diligence

*But by the grace of God I am what I am,
and his grace to me was not without effect.
No, I worked harder than all of them– yet
not I, but the grace of God that was with
me. —1 Corinthians 15:10*

There is victory over procrastination through
God's grace. God's grace not only works to "look
past our faults and see our needs," it empowers us for
the work God has ordained in us. God's grace helps
us to be that which we were meant to be.

How does grace work in our lives? The answer to
this question is simple and well-known: grace works
through faith. It is significant that the preposition
here is "through" rather than "by." If grace worked
"by faith" the power of it would come from our faith.
Yet the power is not in we who are fragile, but God
who is all-powerful. Thus whether we waver, falter
or fail, God grace is yet available.

How does grace save us from procrastination? The
power of procrastination is the belief that we cannot
handle the task in front of us. It may be too many little details or seem like too much work. You may
have started too late in the day or feel too distracted.
God's grace gives you power to start, power to go on,
and power to finish as you trust that God will see you
through your shortfalls and limitations. As you consider God's grace, it revives you inwardly. As you

trust it, God works all things together for good.

This understanding has helped me tremendously and I hope it encourages you.

Taking A Stand

Do your best to come to me quickly.
—2 Timothy 4:9

Jesus urged us to love each other as he loved us. (John 15) He said, "By this all men will know that you are my disciples, if you love one another" (John 13:35). We must learn to take a stand for each other.

Once when I was a boy, I had a friend with a little sister. We both thought she was annoying and he voiced this sentiment often. One day I verbally agreed and added a few things as well. "Do not talk about my sister!" he snapped back. This took me back and I returned, "You just got finished talking about her!" I have never forgotten his response: "I can talk about my sister, but you be quiet."

In the church it is sometimes hard to get along. We distance ourselves one from another to avoid conflict. But, we must learn to stand up for one another. Though we may disagree with our brethren, we must stick up for them because they are brethren. Though they are different, or far off, we must still take a stand for them. Remember the words of the apostle: "keep the unity of the Spirit." Be encouraged.

The Mission

Pray also for me, that whenever I open my mouth, words may be given me so that I will fearlessly make known the mystery of the gospel. —Ephesians 6:19-20

Everyone has a role to play in the spread of the gospel. We all need to fulfill this by sharing our faith. Beyond this most basic commitment, we should support full-time Christian workers.

Ask yourself, in what way is your church directly supporting global evangelism? How is the ministry you are a part of playing a part in reaching the world for Christ? How are you personally helping in the process?

The Kingdom is a business and our yearly reports lately have been disappointing. Though many give their lives to Christ, there is yet so much work to do. Dear friends of mine shared with me a case in southern African where thousands upon thousands have given their lives to Christ. They are in need of training, but the laborers are so few and the prayer support in so small.

Every church should participate in praying, sending and giving. I encourage you to grasp this truth. Do not let what you cannot do stop you from doing what you can. Learn about missions to the cities and countries of our world. Pray for global outreach. Teach others to start seeing the world.

Be encouraged.
"The world is my parish"—John Wesley

My Cup Runs Over

You prepare a table before me in the presence of my enemies. You anoint my head with oil; my cup overflows. —Psalm 23:5

God's wants to pour out abundance in our lives. He desires for the cups of our blessings to run over.

When our blessings come, we should be prepared. If we are not prepared, we will spend them on our own passions and miss the opportunity to bless someone else. It is utter foolishness to pour our precious blessing in the black hole of self-gratification. We should sow our blessings into the kingdom so that we can be fruitful and useful in our lives.

We should not be haphazard in our outpouring of blessings. Be wise and sow into what will best advance the kingdom. Form partnerships with others who have been blessed and give strategically. Develop a giving plan and pray God supply for your giving agenda.

Beloved, we have many fields of service both here and abroad that need our prayers and gifts. Ask the Lord to lead you and give your committed support to the advance of the Kingdom! Be encouraged.

Race Rules

There is neither Jew nor Greek, slave nor free, male nor female, for you are all one in Christ Jesus. If you belong to Christ, then you are Abraham's seed, and heirs according to the promise. —Galatians 3:28-29

One of the most confusing, divisive and destructive issues facing modern times is the issue of race. It is fraught with seeds of offense, hatred and malice. Like the common cold it virulently attacks human sensibilities and has no natural cure. Yet, there is a supernatural one.

The strength of racism is confusion and deception. Ignorance and prejudice pervert our natural sense of self-preservation. It stems from ancient myths about humanity—myths that are often more persuasive than truth. What is Red or Black or White? On one hand, symbols of beauty and poise; on the other, foreboding emblems of human sinfulness.

There is no natural cure for racism. Our sinfulness will always pervert our efforts, though they are valiant. Racism stems from sin and is sin. The only hope for the world in this is Christ and the freedom he gives us from sin and the fear of death. Only the reality of his power and promises can free a soul from racism's debilitating touch. How? You can begin to understand by reading Romans 6:13.

Be encouraged.

Running the Race

*Yet for us there is but one God, the Father,
from whom all things came and for whom
we live; and there is but one Lord, Jesus
Christ, through whom all things came and
through whom we live. —1 Corinthians 8:6*

"For us there is but one God . . . ." This is the truth that can set us free from divisive racism in the body of Christ. We cannot deny that pervasive in the church is an "us" and "them" mentality regarding race. How we handle this will determine our ultimate effectiveness for the Kingdom in our world.

Too many of us actively "run the race." We assert the importance of unity in Christ's body, but inwardly we favor one group over the other. This is like a "rat race" in the Kingdom—only, no matter who the winners are, they will still be rats. God has called us for greater things than this.

We must realize the truth. The God that gave them life, is our Father. The God that blessed "us" with what we have is their Father. And, indeed, what we all have belongs to our Father. All things come from Him and through Christ. I believe the Spirit is quickening this truth in the Church and pray He complete it soon.

Be encouraged.

Ambition

Go to the ant, you sluggard; consider its ways and be wise! —Proverbs 6:6

Ambition is important when exercised with a sense of balance. Without ambition, we will never stretch ourselves and will often embrace complacency. Yet, with "too much" ambition—or, the wrong kind of ambition—we become obsessive and boorish. We must develop balance to keep the light of life pure in our eyes.

The Bible says, "go to the ant." Ants have a balanced ambition. Each drone ant has its role to play and it does so with great diligence and determination. Yet, should a fellow worker fall away, the drone knows to "take up the slack." Ants have something in them that drives them forward while never losing sight of the larger purpose.

What are your ambitions? Are they significant? Are they balanced? God has placed something in you to drive you. It is not about status or pride. You have a role to play. Be encouraged.

Integrity in Adversity

They repay me evil for good and leave my soul forlorn. Yet when they were ill, I put on sackcloth and humbled myself with fasting. —Psalm 35:12-13

The Bible teaches us to repay evil with good. (Rom. 12:17-21) Your ability to do this is the measure of your integrity.

Integrity is your ability to hold to your principles whatever the situation. It requires faith, for you can only hold firm to what is right when trust that God will be pleased and will back you up.

A show of integrity is a show of grace and strength. It sets you apart. It is a prerequisite for adulthood. Truly, it is the mettle of our spiritual maturity. We prove our integrity in adversity and trial. Sometimes we do not pass the test, but if we value our integrity, we will be more determined to pass it the next time.

Be strong in tough times, and be encouraged.

By Faith

...through whom we have gained access by faith into this grace in which we now stand. —Roman 5:2

There is a real and explicit power that God gives us when we become Christians. The Bible calls this power "grace" or "favor." This power enables us to live as God would have us.

Paul says that we stand through the power of grace. Peter talks of partaking in the divine nature through holding firm the promises (favor) of God. (2 Pet. 1:4) He witnesses to the power of the Holy Spirit to purge our conscience and guard of lives. (1 Pet. 1:2) Our Lord Jesus declares that we are like branches as he is the vine. (John 15:1) There is a definite power by which we live in Christ.

Faith accesses this power. To say that we have "gained access" means that this power is available to us in Christ. We must appropriate it. Just because we have access to something does not mean it will automatically take effect in our lives. We are justified by faith, but we must also live day by day by faith.

See!

Hear, you deaf; look, you blind, and see!
—Isaiah 42:18

Few things are more frustrating than not being able to see. When I wear my glasses after a time without them, how much I could not see amazes me. I once heard of a story of a little boy who got glasses for the first time—he stared at himself in a mirror for about fifteen minutes. We can often take the gift of sight for granted, both natural sight and spiritual sight.

The Word of God gives us corrected spiritual sight. Study of the Word is like wearing your glasses. If we think we can go without it, we delude ourselves. We need God's Word to see the truth correctly.

So much of what we go through is based on simple problems. So much goes wrong because we see things improperly—not through the lense of God's Word. Whether it is conflict or loss or challenge or trial, if we would wear our spiritual glasses, we could see our way through. I encourage you today to realize what you may be missing. See God's way. Bless you.

Breaking Through

If only they were wise and would under-stand this and discern what their end will be! —Deuteronomy 32:29

We must understand the climate of this nation. We have become drunk with our success and in many ways it is killing us. The Bible says, "Whoever loves discipline loves knowledge, but he who hates correction is stupid" (Prov. 12:1). We are a people who have thrown off restraint. We extol grandeur and show, whether in the world or in the word, but chafe and hiss at discipline and guidance.

I have a sobering word. Your comfort and ease may be killing you. How often does the Lord speak to you before you listen? How often will you have to hear the right thing to do before you do it?

I have seen the ravages of this disease called ease, or complacency. Honestly I sometimes relapse into the throes of this sickness. Yet, God's healing and grace-filled words repeatedly lift me, saying simply, "trust and obey."

Beloved, heed this advice given by God before you lose more of what is sacred to you. There is a real and powerful breakthrough for you . . . only believe! Be encouraged.

The Spirit of Privilege

Rejoice and be glad, because great is your reward in heaven, for in the same way they persecuted the prophets who were before you. —Matthew 5:12

We are to have the Holy Spirit. This is the heritage of the prophets of old. In times past, God poured out His Spirit only on a few men and women. These men and women exampled extraordinary ability. Now He has done something even more radical. God has poured out His Spirit on all flesh.

We are privileged to partake of the great blessing that for centuries was limited to an elite few. As we have taken on Christ, he has given us the Holy Spirit. This is amazing! Because of God's direct presence in our lives, radical and extraordinary things can happen in and through us.

We cannot discount this tremendous gift! We must not. Learn to count more on the power of the Spirit in your life. Do not cut yourself short. The privilege of God's Spirit resident in you calls you to great things. I encourage you today to realize what you really know deep down inside.

Look

After this I looked, and there before me was a door standing open in heaven.
—Revelation 4:1

God has laid open many doors in your life, but you must look to see them. Do not presume God will both open the doors for you and then make you look for them. Looking for God's hand in your life is an act of faith. It is your responsibility.

Looking is a function of faith. Just as when you look for a lost item, the process is sometimes long and sometimes very short. It all depends on the situation. When you walk by faith, walk looking for what God is doing around you. Be careful not to give up too quickly when you look.

I encourage you today in your faith. Never treat faith as some kind of magic, pulling miracles out of God. Faith is going to our loving Father with specific needs and trusting Him to work things out the way that is best for us. The former is really not faith at all. The latter is the response of love and trust that God expects from us.

Be encouraged.

Mercy, Mercy Me

But go and learn what this means: 'I desire mercy, not sacrifice.' For I have not come to call the righteous, but sinners.
—Matthew 9:13

God is seeking sinners. Broken, wounded, shifty, shiftless, hardheaded, unwieldy, stubborn, dirty, drunken, immoral, thieving, lying, cheating, gossiping, hurting: He is seeking all sinners. God wants people like this to be His people.

God wants the prostitute, the drug-dealer, and the drug-user. He wants those in the nightlife and in the "thug life." He wants the embezzling executive, the adulterous assistant, the abusive husband, the conniving wife. He calls the cold racist, the murderous youth, and the abominable rapist. He wants the war-crazed politician, businessperson using child labor and the race-profiling police officer. He wants the homosexual and the homophobic. He wants the profane rap artist and the amoral R&B star. He wants the father who was not there. He wants the mother who did not care. He wants the violent teen and the hateful little child. Have you winced yet?

God wants to show His mercy is sufficient, whatever the sin. He wants to show it through you. He wants to bless the one that curses you today. This is not to neglect you. It is because He has already taken care of you in spite of your sin and now wants to do the same for someone else. Blessed be the God of mercy, who had mercy on you and on me!

The Game

For our struggle is not against flesh and blood, but against the rulers, against the authorities, against the powers of this dark world and against the spiritual forces of evil in the heavenly realms. —Ephesians 6:12

Things in our world can be very confusing. Many of us are plagued with the nagging sense that things are just not what they used to be. Everything is spinning out of control. Often we can numb ourselves to these senses, but ever more wake up calls are coming our way. What do we do in a world such as ours?

Let me be honest with you. The way things are in these days is no accident. A very organized adversary is at large, pulling loose strings from the fabrics of our lives. The chaos around us is not random. It is intentional, and we must struggle against it.

My joy is knowing however that we do not struggle alone. The God who "works all things together for good" is yet in charge. Our part is not to struggle against all evil, life or death, if you will. It is much more simple. Our part is to stand in the truth of our victory.

I charge you, therefore, to stand and never to let up in your walk with Christ. Keep your Bible reading and studying going. Stay prayed up. When your discipline lacks, do not trip—get back up again. Know that God has your back. Most of all, always and at all times, be encouraged.

Made to Hunger

*He humbled you, causing you to hunger
and then feeding you with manna, which
neither you nor your fathers had known, to
teach you that man does not live on bread
alone but on every word that comes from
the mouth of the Lord. —Deuteronomy 8:3*

Without spiritual hunger we have no means of attaining true spiritual nourishment. Spiritual hunger gives us the impulse to strengthen our spiritual lives. It works much like our physical hunger.

When we are not hungry, we are not likely to eat. Have you ever noticed how difficult force-feeding yourself on God's Word is? For some, keeping up with daily devotional is like dragging oneself on gravel. We should never read the Word because it is our duty or just to keep up our religion. When we read or pray, we should do it out of hunger.

What should we do when we do not feel hungry? Scripture helps us understand that God "makes us to hunger" so that He can feed us with His spiritual food. Spiritual hunger comes from God.

We gain and maintain spiritual hunger through worship, right perspective and godly confessions. These three work together. Seek after God through these means and you will be encouraged.

Hunger and Worship

Worship the Lord your God, and his bless-
ing will be on your food and water. I will
take away sickness from among you.
—Exodus 23:25

When we live a healthy and normal Christian life, God works a hunger for His Word, for prayer and other spiritual things. Without spiritual hunger, our walk with God becomes very difficult. One means of gaining this spiritual hunger is through worship.

Worship is the act of giving God glory. It is done with our body, soul and spirit. It is expressed with our hands, feet, arms, hearts, mouths, tears, cries, shouts; it is done through actions like rocking, weeping, leaping, waving, bowing, prostrating (lying out on the floor in utter submission), keeping silence, dancing, running, hugging, abasing (see Rev. 4:10), giving, singing, praying and prophesying (see I Sam. 19:19-24). When we worship, we make our inward affirmation an outward expression. The Holy Spirit makes it possible as He communes with our very spirit. (Rom. 8:16)

Sometimes our feelings run haywire and it seems God is not near. Yet, God's Word affirms that He never leaves us and the Spirit gives us a sense that He is still with us. When we worship, we affirm this truth and bring our feelings into submission to the truth.

Worship brings spiritual hunger in one or two ways. When we get spiritually numb or weary of keeping spiritual disciplines, worship reignites us to spiritual things and refreshes our hunger. If our walk is already lively, constant worship will keep our spiritual drive and engine well oiled.

I encourage you, seek the Lord through the act of giving glory to His Name.

Speaking the Truth

It is written: "I believed; therefore I have spoken." With that same spirit of faith we also believe and therefore speak.
—2 Corinthians 4:13

We know and experience truth more through faith than by fact. It was once a fact that the sun circled the earth. People once lived and died by the fact that the earth was flat. Yet, these facts led us not to truth, but deception.

There are many facts of life, but not all of them help us live in the truth. Many facts about our individual lives are used to define us, but they are not true at all. Beloved, God's Word is the truth. It is not your circumstance, job, status, past, or even your gifts and abilities that truly define you—God's Word does.

When we experience truth, we hunger for more. Yet we cannot experience the truth if we live by just the facts. What we believe is evident by what we speak. The truth is, two things are vying for the attention of our lives: our flesh and our spirit. If we speak the opinion of our flesh, we will live by it. If we speak the expression of the Spirit in faith, this will control our lives.

Be careful what you say. God loves you and always has a wonderful plan for you. Encourage yourself with the truth and be encouraged.

The Day of Freedom

I saw thrones on which were seated those who had been given authority to judge.
—Revelation 20:4

A day of freedom is coming! A proper understanding of what God has in store for believers will set fire to our souls. Such a vision of God's reward made early Christians willing to go through unimaginable obstacles for the sake of righteousness. May this motivation now be revived in us.

Do not let popular culture dominate your mind. Its imaginations regarding heaven and eternity are false. The Bible teaches of a day of reckoning where God will reward believers for what is done in Jesus' name in this life. We will receive an inheritance of great and wonderful things that are better than the best this world can offer.

Of what will our inheritance consist? When Jesus returns, he will turn the tables on the powerful and wicked. He will take their great riches and possessions from them and pass them to we who wait patiently for him. Those ridiculed and persecuted for what is true and right, will be vindicated and rewarded. On the Day of Freedom, the "first shall be last and the last first."

I encourage you, beloved, press for the prize. It will be hard and you may face difficulties and losses as you stand for Christ. Know that all God's prophets and Christ himself faced the same. Great will be your reward when Christ pours out the abundant inheritance.

Be encouraged.

Doing What's Right

And without faith it is impossible to please God, because anyone who comes to him must believe that he exists and that he rewards those who earnestly seek him.
—Hebrews 11:6

Too many Christians live defeated lives. They know what is right, but they do not do it. This grieves God's heart—and not for all the reasons that we might think.

Three things are important in our walk with God and these are they: hearing God call us, answering the call and fulfilling it. Many of us are good at hearing God's call and some of us answer. We come to know His will and set ourselves up to do it. For instance, we join a church and even get involved in the Bible Studies and activities. This positioning is necessary, but stopping here is dangerously wrong.

We must not only know what is right. We must do it. The "doing" often creates a crisis of belief and calls for major adjustments. However, not to do what God expects is sin and a sign of faulty faith.

No one can say that they truly love God and forsake His Word. If we believe He is who He says He is, then we will earnestly seek to please Him. We will put Him first in every aspect of our lives. He will get our best. If our faith does not motivate us to do what is right, it is a faulty faith, riddled with deception.

Beloved, it is the truth that makes us free. Be free today and be encouraged.

Making Ends Meet

Be very careful, then, how you live– not as unwise but as wise, making the most of every opportunity, because the days are evil. —Ephesians 5:15-16

God calls us to "redeem the time." We are living in evil days. We are not just living in bad times, we are living in evil days. When this revelation soaks in our hearts, we will surely make the most of every opportunity.

The difference between "bad times" and "evil days" is subtle, but major. Bad times come to pass. The phrase speaks of an unfortunate moment in history, rather than a terminal condition of society. There is no judgement for bad times—"bad things happen." In bad times, we simply brace ourselves and look for better times to come.

We are not living in bad times but are living in evil days. Evil days come to "steal, kill and destroy," if you will. They speak of murder, malice and mayhem and point to the sickness passed from one generation to another. This sickness will not just go away; we must fight against it, lest it infect—if it were possible—even the elect of God.

The days are evil and we must be wise. We must learn to set priorities and focus on God's business. We must make ends meet—not worldly ends, but spiritual ones. We must turn our attention from seeking wealth and happiness to seeking God's kingdom. What is the difference? I can tell you, but then you would have to kill your flesh. . .

Boldness for Christ

Pray also for me, that whenever I open my mouth, words may be given me so that I will fearlessly make known the mystery of the gospel, for which I am an ambassador in chains. Pray that I may declare it fearlessly, as I should. —Ephesians 6:19-20

It takes boldness to walk in the Lord. You cannot walk in Christ and walk in fear at the same time—each cancels the other out. Remember the admonition, "God has not given you a spirit of fear."

When God saved you He gave you the grace and power to walk with Him. Yet, you must exert the faith to walk in this power. You must trust that when you move to do what God expects, you will find the strength in the journey. You will not find it "before," but "in." Thus, you must boldly stand on God's Word and what it calls you to do.

Even when obeying God imperils your life, you must take on the mantle of boldness. Paul had mighty experiences of God and declared unremittingly their glory and worth; yet, he describes the experiences like this: "For we who are alive are always being given over to death for Jesus' sake, so that his life may be revealed in our mortal body." (2 Cor. 4:11)

You must be bold. Overcome your fears of loss or pain. Find strength in the journey. Steal away from your sinfulness, knowing that God has what is better for you. Give your flesh over to death and experience God's real and tangible "exceeding abundance." Will you not be bold today?

Be encouraged.

What's Best?

Whoever can be trusted with very little can also be trusted with much, and whoever is dishonest with very little will also be dishonest with much. —Luke 16:10

"And now I will show you the most excellent way" (1 Cor. 12:31). The life of a Christian is a life of standard. It bears purpose. It is a life worth living. Yet, we do not all walk in excellence and, as we go through these last days, we are failing to walk in it more and more.

Excellence is built on little things. Consider, for instance, what makes a good poem. Nuance, choice words, and punctuation are all important. What makes a good song? Phraseology, articulation, or the slightest improvisation at the rarest moment makes it unforgettable. The difference between a president and any other leader is pomp and circumstance. The difference between a good parent and a bad one is undivided attention and care. The difference between a high and low level executive is grooming. The difference between a talented athlete and an Olympian is attention to detail.

Do not let the world rob you for your excellence. Do not be denied to live the life worth living. True, we will never be "there"; we will never be perfect—but, excellence has nothing to do with perfection. Be faithful in the little things and do not be discouraged.

The Politics of Jesus

Be completely humble and gentle; be patient, bearing with one another in love.
—Ephesians 4:2

The church is irrevocably political. Politics deal with how people relate to each other. No matter the system or structure, politics will always be involved. Considering this fact, we each must come to understand the politics of Jesus.

When Jesus stood before Pilate, the Roman procurator demanded he speak and defend himself. Jesus spoke nothing. Pilate demanded again, insisting on his ability to control whether Christ would live or die. Jesus in turn responded brilliantly. He answered, "You would have no power over me if it were not given to you from above" (John 19:11).

Politics are often about control. The politics of Jesus begins with understanding that God is in control. God will intervene and make the difference if we walk in His way. Let us learn how to rest in Him and know as we walk in the Spirit, He will fight our battles.

Be encouraged.

Amazing Doubt

And he was amazed at their lack of faith.
—Mark 6:6

God is calling every Christian to be a leader. Leadership is our intended, "natural" state. (See Gen. 1:26-31) We are to stand as lights in this dark world, even when our light exposes great evil and places us at risk. Godly leadership requires a firmness of faith. However, we live in a "weak-faith" age and our current leadership is weak.

Always address problems at the root. Our leadership falters because our faith does and our faith is weak because we treat Jesus commonly. Note this. Jesus worked mighty miracles in every place he went, except in his hometown. The people were too familiar with him. They had seen him grow up and had known his family. This is interesting. Better than anyone else in history, they could verify his sinless character, his virgin-birth, and other remarkable attributes. Instead they used their familiarity with him to relegate him to "just one of Mary's boys."

We, especially those saved for a long time, are also very familiar with Jesus in this way. We sin and say, "I know he will forgive me." We give less than our best and say, "the Lord knows my heart." We lose our sense of wonder, thinking that we have seen it all before. When we hear the Word in its freshness, it hits us like an old dry familiar tune.

Wake up, dear friends, to the call! This generation needs leadership—our leadership! Your specialness, your gift, your God-inspired message, must come forward! But, we need a firmness inspired by amazed faith. Be encouraged, lest we amaze Jesus with our doubt.

Enter In!

Your wives, your children and your live-stock may stay in the land that Moses gave you east of the Jordan, but all your fighting men, fully armed, must cross over ahead of your brothers. You are to help your brothers. —Joshua 1:14

Many of us are staying in the "land that Moses gave us." By this I mean that we have begun growing spiritually, but have not entered our purpose. Think on this carefully. What would have happened if Christ had denied his purpose and just come, healing and working miracles? The answer, of course, is obvious. It is just as bad when we get spiritual and neglect to move into our call.

I encourage you, friends, do not be satisfied with "big churches" and large ministries. Exciting worship and the gifts of the spirit are both good things. But, these are a means to an end, not an end in themselves.

God has brought us out of confining tradition and religion to take us into something else. Do not be satisfied with being brought out! Enter into God's call! He has raised us in this critical time to reap the greatest spiritual harvest ever. The Kingdom of Heaven is at hand my friends.

Be encouraged.

Set Apart

Paul, a servant of Christ Jesus, called to be an apostle and set apart for the gospel of God . . . —Romans 1:1

Paul was an effective soul-winner and motivator of soul-winners. The churches he planted grew as his intensity fueled them. He saw himself as one completely set apart for the gospel, as others followed his example.

It is not hard to "think gospel." You simply need a bit of knowledge and a clear vision of the mission. The gospel is making a difference throughout the world, saving souls from darkness and preparing a people to receive the Great King. Our mission is to teach the nations about Christ and his way, calling people to obey him and to a wonderful new life.

This mission is powerfully being accomplished throughout the world. Search out how well the mission goes where you are— in your city, in your church, in your own life.

Be set apart and be encouraged.

Good Living

"Why do not you judge for yourselves what is right? —Luke 12:57

What exasperates Jesus? When his people know what is right and stubbornly refuse it. This is the case for many of us.

God has done more than bend over backwards to bring us into what is right. The Bible says He is "the compassionate and gracious God, slow to anger, abounding in love and faithfulness" (Ex. 34:6). He has given us His grace and stayed His anger. This will not last forever.

We will not escape God wrath if we ignore His grace. It is one thing to do wrong and another to slap the hand that would help us turn around. The Bible also says He "does not leave the guilty unpunished; he punishes the children and their children for the sin of the fathers to the third and fourth generation." To protect His divine plan, He will punish the guilty who remain when His grace is expended.

Jesus' exasperation comes from knowing all God has sacrificed to help us and seeing our complacency and continued disobedience. The heart of God pleads for us to be restored. He says to us "If you will return, O Israel, return to me" (Jer. 4:1). Hear the heart of God. Turn and do what you what you know is right and honor God's faith in you.

Be encouraged.

When Was the Last Time You Cried?

Record my lament; list my tears on your scroll– are they not in your record?
—Psalm 56:8

When was the last time you cried? Where were you? Were you with others, or by yourself? Beloved, these questions are so important to the issue of holiness and godliness. How you handle sorrow, disappointment and travail will ultimately affect how you live your life.

The Bible teaches us a healthy way to handle sadness. Sorrow has many causes and God has an answer for each. Every tear carries the message of our sorrow to Him and He records them in a book. As we cry, we pray and God hears every phrase.

Nowhere in the Bible does it advocate "putting on a good face" for everybody and covering up your sorrow. Time and again, just the opposite is shown. When should we cry? There is a time and a place. Find a quiet time and a place of prayer. Do not always go it alone. Call a trustworthy friend.

Do not practice "holding things in." God is with you and sweeps up every tear to place in a special bottle. He will always provide and never let you be alone.

Be encouraged.

Getting It Right

If you do what is right, will you not be accepted? But if you do not do what is right, sin is crouching at your door; it desires to have you, but you must master it.
—*Genesis 4:7*

Life is very dangerous, living in the gray. Consider the life of Cain. When Cain was young, no one could have told him he would kill his brother, Abel. Cain was a hard-working man. Maybe he was a good father and a good husband. But, murder found access into his heart because he lived a compromised life.

Do not pride yourself on the wrong you did not do. When you know what is right to do and do it not, you sin. (Jas. 4:17) It is easy to slip into wrongdoing when you are not committed to doing what is right.

Our lives must stand for something again. Let us step out of the gray blasé of "anything goes." Sin waits at the door and we must become masters over it.

Be encouraged.

Servanthood

Not so with you. Instead, whoever wants to become great among you must be your servant, and whoever wants to be first must be your slave. —Matthew 20:26-27

The secret to leadership is servanthood. The key to inspiration is commitment to others. Praying often that God would give you more of a servant's heart. Seek to be first by God's estimate, not the world's.

Think on Paul the apostle. Paul lived his life to the fullest. No other mortal man in history can claim to have lived more completely than Paul. His life was filled with struggles and tests, but he joyfully overcame them all. The key to his success was that he chose to make his suffering useful.

When we live a life of service to others, we redeem our suffering. We make everything we do and experience in life meaningful. I would rather suffer seeking justice for the poor, than be miserable in my comfort. I would rather struggle to make things better, than sit helplessly and watch the world fall apart.

Servanthood makes life worth living. "Lord, create in me a servant heart!"

Be encouraged.

A Servant's Heart

*So you also, when you have done every-
thing you were told to do, should say, "We
are unworthy servants; we have only done
our duty." —Luke 17:10*

Whatever is in our hearts is what comes up and
out. We can try to cover up the bad things in our
hearts, but they will become known eventually. The
person with a good heart will be known as well. This
is why it is important to have a servant's heart.
Acting like a servant just will not do. Eventually our
true nature will shine forth. We must be servants at
heart.

A servant's heart is pure. It is singleminded in purpose. A servant's heart is honest. It seeks to give true
assistance, not just an appearance of such. A servant's heart is bold and courageous. It is ignited with
godly anger at injustice and sin. A servant's heart is
humble. It forsakes its own glory and is ashamed
should self-seeking arise in it. A servant's heart is
righteous. Common opinion does not satisfy it. It
seeks what is right according to the truth. A servant's
heart is inspirational. Others around it easily catch it.

I encourage you, do not just serve, be a servant.
Let your life be poured out for others in every way.
When you do this, you will know what Paul meant
by the phrase, "To live is Christ."

Be encouraged.

The Good Servant

You, my brothers, were called to be free. But do not use your freedom to indulge the sinful nature; rather, serve one another in love. —Galatians 5:13

A foremost trait of the true servant is eagerness. A good servant does not serve reluctantly. He or she is set to look out for the needs of others. Eagerness speaks of initiative and forwardness. It is a sign of true love.

In Charles Swindoll's book, *Improving Your Serve*, he speaks of the philosophy of a servant resting upon two principles: "defenselessness" and eagerness. He wonderfully explains the first in the phrase, "nothing to lose, nothing to prove." True service focuses on others and not ourselves.

The second principle, however, struck me. Eagerness. Beloved, we should be eager to find every opportunity we can to serve others. We should look out for them with expectancy and excitement. Why? Servanthood enables us to walk as Christ walked and, by this, to experience Christ more meaningfully in our lives. These rewards are very substantive.

As always, dear friends, be encouraged.

Nothing to Lose, Nothing to Prove

For whoever wants to save his life will lose it, but whoever loses his life for me and for the gospel will save it. —Mark 8:35

Jesus makes it abundantly clear in his Word that in serving him we have nothing to lose and nothing to prove.

Sometimes, we neglect to serve others for fear of someone taking advantage of us. We fear we will lose face or worse. God does not give us this spirit of fear. He gives us power to love others with a sound mind. (2 Tim. 1:7)

I encourage you today, let nothing stop you from exercising the privilege God has given you to serve. Remember Joseph who served his way from a prison to a palace. Remember Daniel who served his way from exile to exultation. Remember Paul who served his way through persecution and trial to spread the gospel across the western world.

Christ came to serve, not to be served. Should we experience Christ profoundly in our lives, we must be like him. We must serve unreservedly. For what profit is it to save face—to save honor—to save pride—to save our very lives, and to forfeit the blessing of our very souls? Be encouraged.

. . . *As Unto the Lord*

Fear the Lord your God, serve him only and take your oaths in his name.
—Deuteronomy 6:13

Everything we do should be "as unto the Lord." The Bible gives us ample instruction regarding our attitude and motivation for work and service.

Everybody should, in whatever position they are in, see themselves as a servant. Employees should not "cheat the system," but should serve their employers as unto the Lord. Children should not roll their eyes in rebellion. They should be taught to be strong servants. Ministers should lead by serving the Lord and the people for His sake.

God has set you where you are to accomplish a specific and particular objective. You are there not for your own success, but for His. Your life is tied to a greater purpose. You must think about how you are handling yourself. Are you serving Christ's purpose in the midst? Remember the words of the Scripture and take them seriously: "Serve wholeheartedly, as if you were serving the Lord, not men." (Eph. 6:7)

Be encouraged.

The Gift of Serving

If it is serving, let him serve. *—Romans 12:7*

This message extols the most honored people in Christ. Jesus said that the greatest in His kingdom would be the servants of all others.

Serving others is a calling for every Christian. We should all become experts this. Yet, there are those who serve the servers. They are support people and help others do what they do best. Sometimes we call them armorbearers or special assistants. Most times they bear no title, have no particular position, and are rarely acknowledged.

Think about who comes early to open the church and sees to it that it is locked tight when everyone is gone. Think about who arranges the room in which we have our meetings. Think about those that come after service and pick up the papers we have patently scattered across the pews. Think about those that make up for our carelessness, cover our busyness, polish our brashness, sweeten our curtness, follow up when we forget and pick us up when we get weary.

Often these are the most forgotten persons in the church. They miss the limelight by design, trusting in a much greater reward. Beloved, honor them today. These will be the people that we will serve when Christ's Kingdom comes in its fullness.

Rewards for the Servant

I tell you the truth, he will put him in charge of all his possessions. —Matthew 24:47

A servant's reward is a greater opportunity to serve. True servants understand that fulfillment comes from serving God and others. They know what Jesus meant by "it is better to give than to receive" and "he that wants to be greatest must become the servant of all."

Jesus rewards us when we take our small tasks of obedience to him and complete them with zeal and forthrightness. These tasks make small contributions to his overall plan and usually make more of a difference in us than anywhere else. They are training runs. When we are faithful, he rewards us with greater opportunities to make a difference. As we proceed faithfully through the tasks he assigns, we leave a wonderful legacy in the kingdom and can be gratified by the significance God has added to our lives.

I encourage you to take seriously whatever God has placed in front of you right now. When you seek to please God in little things, He will grant greater opportunities for you to be used to bring glory to the Kingdom and win greater rewards in heaven.

As always, be encouraged.

Inspiring Service

He must become greater; I must become less. —John 3:30

Service is the heartbeat of God. We also must develop a heart for it. Anyone can act like a servant, but being a servant is only for those who are willing to pay the cost.

First, you must be God's servant. You must be born again and committed to Christlikeness. You accomplish this primarily through prayer, praise, worship and an openness to listen and learn.

Second, you must serve others. Learn to see the needs of others, whatever shape, form or age. Put their needs first and trust God to take care of yours. Seek your reward and pleasure from God.

Lastly, you must play your part. Everyone has a specific role in God's work. We learn our "call" best when we start serving others in general. When you seek after your call, it should not be to fulfill yourself. Learn how to put others first in general practice, and God will mature you for your special work.

Unending Service

Live as free men, but do not use your free-
dom as a cover-up for evil; live as servants
of God. —1 Peter 2:16

We must remember that God has called us to both freedom and service. It is our service that makes us truly free. The life lived without the spirit of serving is never free. With this understanding, never stop serving.

Serving is like worship. It is to be done in spirit and truth. We do not serve for others to see us. Our servanthood is in response to the working of God's Spirit and power in our lives.

Do not turn your heart on and off to the spirit of serving others. Serve simply and be gratified by nothing else than the joy and reward of obedience.

Learn the difference between serving for self and serving for purpose—worldly serving and godly serving. Know that the former is self-gratifying, while the latter pleases God. Avoid using your freedom in Christ to serve your own selfish needs. If you cannot see a commitment to unending service, seek for it until it is yours. Be encouraged.

The Victory of Faith

For everyone born of God overcomes the world. This is the victory that has overcome the world, even our faith. —1 John 5:4

You were born for victory. Your assurance of this is like an unbreakable chassis fortifying your walk with God. The victory has not been won by your strength or passion. It was won for you by an unbeatable Champion. Victory is in our life because of God's grace through the Lord Jesus Christ.

We experience Christ's victory for our lives through faith. Unfortunately, we often have the wrong idea about faith and miss what God has for us. We too often consider it with reference to our convenience or pleasure. Faith has nothing to do with making this world convenient for us.

My friends, we often miss the true riches of faith and the very glory of God in our pursuit of worldly comforts. In plain words, "you have to go through it to get to it." Faith is our trust in God that helps us face and overcome life's challenges.

I urge you today to forsake whatever love affair with the world you may have. Let the Lord take you through uncomfortable places. Learn to raise Him in tight spots. Only then can you know true victory. Victory is overcoming tough odds, not avoiding them.

Be encouraged.

Love the Word

...because we have heard of your faith in Christ Jesus and of the love you have for all the saints–the faith and love that spring from the hope that is stored up for you in heaven and that you have already heard about in the word of truth, the gospel.
—Colossians 1:4-5

God's Word contains power for living. We should not shortchange it. The Bible has more to offer than we oftentimes think.

Why do you read the Bible? What do you gain from studying it? You can try to be as comprehensive as you like. You will never fully answer these questions. God has put eternity in Holy Writ and you will never exhaust what it has to offer.

God powerfully reminded me of this once. I had been led to read several chapters during morning and evening sessions—a pattern prescribed in Scriptures (Ps. 1:1-4). I finished my reading one evening and was rather pleased with myself for keeping up a rigid reading schedule. The word of the Lord came to me and our Father asked if I was satisfied with what I received from the Word that evening. Though I had read quite a bit and fulfilled my obligation, I was not full.

I share this because it is so easy to fulfill set times for devotion and prayer and Bible reading with a sense of duty and accomplishment. This, we do, sometimes forgetting the real reason for immersing ourselves in the Word. We should love it. We should hate when the special time we share with our Father is over. Is this where you are today?

The Beginning of Faith

"Bring the best of the firstfruits of your soil to the house of the Lord your God.
— Exodus 34:26

God and God alone deserves the best and the first. It is only right that we give Him, in the words of Oswald Chambers, "our utmost for His highest—our best for His glory." Giving God what is best is the beginning of our walk of faith.

Giving God what is best involves our heart and our spirit, our attitude and our emotions. The best that comes from the heart, goes to the heart. When we give God the first of what we have, we both put Him first in our lives and we declare that all that we have truly belongs to Him. When we do not give our best, we lack faith and God does not honor our service. (Gen. 4:3-5)

Give God your best and do your best in all you do. Know that you will not always be at your best, but you must always try. If you do not try, know that whatever you are doing is not truly unto the Lord. Let His grace stir in you and you will see His wondrous goodness.

Keep the faith and be encouraged this day.

Is it Faith?

Now faith is being sure of what we hope for and certain of what we do not see.
—Hebrews 11:1

We can conceive Biblical faith as having three dimensions. These comprise three increasing levels of knowing God.

In the first dimension, our faith follows the knowledge that God is. The Bible says even the demons know this and tremble. (Jas. 2:19) This faith produces the reverential fear of the Lord. Yet, if we stop at this level, it will be what the Word calls a "dead faith."

The second dimension involves specific knowledge about God. Here we learn about God's character and His principles (i.e., statutes, ordinances, laws, commands, commandments). Persons exercising this faith are they who not only know that God is, but know "he is a rewarder of those that diligently seek Him." They can "get a prayer through." Yet, they can too easily get tripped up when things seem out of control.

It is in the third dimension that we are "filled with the fullness of God." Paul prayed for all Christians to reach this stage (Eph. 3:16-20). At this "level" we simply know God. No one can easily offend us. (Phil. 1:9-10) Trials do not often scare us. We rest because of His promises, knowing that God will work in us, through us and often in spite of us to bring about His plan. And we know that His plan is to "prosper us and not to harm us."

These levels can be blurred at the borders. Yet may they enhance our understanding of where we want to be in God. Be encouraged.

Take Charge for Your Life

In the same way, count yourselves dead to sin but alive to God in Christ Jesus.
—Romans 6:11

You must take charge of your life. This does not mean you are to be in control of your life. This right belongs to God. Rather, you must take the reigns of your life and do what you know in your spirit to do.

So many of us live in hiding. In our dreams, we see who we really are. In our moments of quiet we become acquainted with ourselves. But, when we go out into the world, we put up a front. It is like going on autopilot. We coast through our days with our acquaintances and coworkers, simply fitting in.

God did not call you to fit in, my beloved friends. The world needs you to be who you really are! The Bible says, "Let Christ dwell in your heart through faith" (Eph. 3:17). Do you know what this means? Christ wants to live through you, activating the gifts he has deposited in you. But, it takes faith, my friends. It takes faith, so be encouraged.

Freshness in God

It has given me great joy to find some of your children walking in the truth, just as the Father commanded us. —2 John 1:4

It is our duty and privilege to remain fresh in God. This is not always the easiest thing to do. What is required for our fire to remain hot is often what we are prone to avoid.

The Bible says the Spirit of God surely rests on us when we are insulted for the name of Christ. (1 Pet. 4:14) Paul exclaimed that he gloried in the trials of the Christian life because such trial led to maturity and spiritual strength. (Rom. 5:1-5) Indeed, our Lord declares through His Word that we are blessed when we are reviled for our faith. (Matt. 5:3-11)

We are prone to avoid the criticism that comes because of our faith in God. Yet, God uses this for our good and strengthens our spirits. Next time you are insulted or offended, take it as affirmation that God's Spirit is with you.

Be encouraged.

Love Perfected

There is no fear in love. But perfect love drives out fear, because fear has to do with punishment. The one who fears is not made perfect in love. —1 John 4:18

Dear friends, "perfect love drives out all fear." It is the power of love that drives us to share the truth of God's love with others.

What should be the focus of our lives? It is to walk in the love of God and to share it with others. (Phil. 1:18-21) When He saves us, God gives us this opportunity for a meaningful and abundant life. (John 10:10) When we do this, we show that the love of God fills us.

Let God's love be perfected in you, friend. Share your testimony. Pray for a coworker. Call a lonely elder. Visit a local school. Support a missionary. Help a family in need. Open your home to new neighbors. Bless a young person in college. Do not be afraid to open up to someone and bless them for the sake of Christ and his love. Be encouraged.

Keep the Sayings

Pay attention and listen to the sayings of the wise; apply your heart to what I teach.
—Proverbs 22:17

Our minds are often a battlefield. On one hand, our fleshly passion vies for control. On the other, we seek to live by godliness, discipline and wisdom. It is a struggle sometimes to do or think what is right, when we have such dominate voices leading us into wrong thinking.

Let me illustrate my point. When a person becomes depressed, they often deal with tremendously negative thinking. Thoughts like "I'm not worth it," "they'll think me a bad person," "I've really messed up now," "I'm not going to make it," etc. bombard our hearts. They do not ask permission and are not easily pushed out of our minds. When they are, they quickly come back.

Remember now the Scripture that says, ". . . we take captive every thought to make it obedient to Christ." (2 Cor. 10:5) How do we do this? By "keeping the sayings." We must read and study the Word of God and speak what it says regarding our lives.

I encourage you, then, today to read and study God's Word often. Seek His face and as you do He will speak to every concern in your life.

Be encouraged.

Hope in the Lord

Heal me, O Lord, and I will be healed; save me and I will be saved, for you are the one I praise. —Jeremiah 17:14

How well do you know the Lord? When we say that we know someone, we mean that we have confidence in their character and in our relationship with them. We can predict their response or actions. Think about a spouse or a good partner at the job. Your working relationship is based on trust and understanding what the other person expects.

God wants us to know Him. A most dynamic principle is this: God is always at work around us and wants us to join him in that work. God wants us to know Him and trust that He will be consistent and faithful in your relationship with Him.

The Bible says:

Therefore, since we have been justified through faith, we have peace with God through our Lord Jesus Christ, through whom we have gained access by faith into this grace in which we now stand. And we rejoice in the hope of the glory of God. Not only so, but we also rejoice in our sufferings, because we know that suffering produces perseverance; perseverance, character; and character, hope. And hope does not disappoint us, because God has poured out his love into our hearts by the Holy Spirit, whom he has given us. (Rom. 5:1-5)

In this Scriptural litany, Paul outlines how we can have peace and hope in the Lord. It often starts with tribulation. But, as we trust God, that tribulation leads to an intimate relationship with God that in turn leads to a greater trust and hope in the Lord.

Notice, the key to the process is "holding firm faith." God will never leave you or forsake you. He is faithful. I know He is. Be encouraged.

The Servant

One of those days Jesus went out to a mountainside to pray, and spent the night praying to God. —Luke 6:12

Verses like this one are like hidden jewels. I cannot count how often I read over verses referring to Jesus praying before I understood their significance. Great value is in understanding the prayer life of Jesus.

The Bible shows us Jesus excelled in every way. Yet he did not lean on his gifts and abilities. He did not make it on his divine wisdom or charisma. Even his miracles and healings were not the main reason his ministry moved. Prayer moved Jesus' work.

If you look, you will notice that before and after each notable miracle, Jesus prayed. He did not ride the wave of opportunity—even God-inspired opportunity. He did not manipulate his way anywhere. Jesus carefully waited for the next step from God in prayer and, even when it seemed crazy, he took it.

Jesus was a servant. He did not seek his own cause. Rather, he kept things simple. He served for God's sake. Go and do likewise.

Be encouraged.

Don't Settle for Just Good

Taste and see that the Lord is good; blessed is the man who takes refuge in him. —Psalm 34:8

Beloved, I write as a desperate man. I am hungry for God. I believe my spiritual walk is good, but, good is just not good enough. What happens when godly order becomes an orchestration? What happens when excitement turns into entertainment? What happens when worship becomes "warm fuzzies?" What happens? Nothing.

Lately I have experienced a deep hunger in my heart. It is a hunger that actually can be passed over easily enough. "Wonderful spiritual experiences" or "dynamic worship services" do not fill it. It is not filled from deep charismatic messages or declarations on a coming revival. These things suffice temporarily, but soon fade away.

Have you ever been handed something that after a short time you simply devalued? Remember those things you yearned for as a child at Christmas—you played with them one day and the next they lost there luster. Even the greatest treasure of all can thus be devalued if we seek it without sacrifice.

The Bible says that if we seek Him, we will find Him if we seek with ALL our hearts and ALL our souls. (Duet. 4:29) I am not seeking just a "warm fuzzy" from God. I want real, sweet communion.

I'm not just looking for the phenomenon, per se, but the honor of His presence. I want real revival, and I want it badly. Is there any that will pray with me?

Faith Walk

We live by faith, not by sight.
—2 Corinthians 5:7

What is the difference between walking by faith and walking by sight? The Bible says, "Trust in the LORD with all your heart; do not depend on your own understanding. Seek His will in all you do, and He will direct your paths" (Prov. 3:5-6, NLT). Walking by faith entails trusting God's direction and care, even when you cannot see your way through.

It takes faith to grow. Growth requires that you successfully face a crisis. Your character is forged by how you handle trouble. When you trust God in hard times, you build good character.

Though faith is not sight, it is not blind. Faith is built on God's Word and promises. We must make the commitment to walk by God's promises and not based on our circumstances. This will give us the fortitude to press through crisis and the stages of faith to maturity. Be encouraged.

Opened Eyes

. . . the oracle of one who hears the words of God, who sees a vision from the Almighty, who falls prostrate, and whose eyes are opened. —Numbers 24:4

This is the spirit of one whose eyes are opened. They are stricken by the holiness of God and they smitten in their hearts. We see God's glory and are wounded. Everyone who truly encounters God comes away with a limp. How I wish we all were inflicted with this blessed wound!

True spiritual sight brands us and renders to us a submitted heart. The Bible says true circumcision is the circumcision of the heart. (Rom. 2:29) Spiritual circumcision is a wounding that brings about submission. We need this in our Christian life as our mark and wound reminding us not to be proud in our ways.

Open your eyes, beloved, and see God for who He truly is. It is time not simply to know about Him, but to know Him. How will you know the difference? When your eyes are truly open, you will bow down. Be encouraged.

Committed

Jesus answered, "I tell you the truth, no one can enter the kingdom of God unless he is born of water and the Spirit. —John 3:5 (NIV)

There is a difference between decision and commitment. Jesus show this in discussing a man who gave instructions to his two sons. The first said he would go but did not. The second said he would not go, but did. (Matt. 21:28-29) Commitment, unlike a simple decision, pertains to follow-through.

When we make decisions, we must be prepared to fulfill them. Preparation is the down-payment of commitment. There is no excuse for not being prepared, for we should not commit to something we are not sure we can do.

The world is short on committed people. We have many who mean well and who want to do good. But few have paid their down-payment. This is a place the people of God can be a witness, for it is a great, great shame for a Christian to fall short of his word. Be different and be encouraged.

Prevailing in Prayer

Then the man said, "Your name will no longer be Jacob, but Israel, because you have struggled with God and with men and have overcome." —Genesis 32:28

I wish to share with you an important lesson I have learned. God did not give Jacob the name, Israel, because He struggled or strived with Him. God gave him that name because he prevailed. There is a difference between struggling and prevailing.

Struggling is inherent in prevailing, but not everyone who struggles prevails. I entertain this point because many of us struggle in our prayer life. Either we struggle to get ourselves to pray, we struggle to keep focus when we pray, or we struggle for the objectives of prayer. These are three different ways or struggling, but the goals for all are a vibrant prayer life and answered prayer.

Many of us must learn to "prevail on God." We must master persistence and learn to pray concerning godly issues and as prompted by the Spirit and not let up until we have gotten an answer. We must seek God for all things and with all our heart and soul. If after a particular time before the Lord your burden remains, catch your breath and go back into the fray. Stay there as long as it takes. If you must interrupt your prayer session for other obligations, remind the Lord as you do what you need to do, and return to focused prayer after you've finished. Do not just struggle, prevail. Expect and answer. Wait for it, cry for it, "fight" for it, press for it. God will give it to those who prevail. Be encouraged.

God is God

Consecrate yourselves and be holy, because I am the Lord your God.
—Leviticus 20:7

The first five books of the Bible are called the Pentateuch, or the "Five Books of Moses." These five books provide a sort of foundation for everything else written in the Scriptures and just about every other book or writing refers back to what they contain. In and through them, God introduces Himself and clarifies to us who He really is.

It is interesting that in the first five books God repeats a phrase time and time again: "I am the LORD your God," "I am the LORD," "I am your God," etc.. This phrase is restated over and again through the Pentateuch and is then repeated many times through the whole Bible. What is the point? God wants us to know Him for who He is.

In reading the story of the great evangelist, Charles Finney, I was stricken with one account that happened days after his conversion to Christ. A great revival had broken out, sparked very much by the Holy Spirit through Finney's conversion, and prayer meetings were being held nightly. Yet, after several days the fervor had begun to wane and Finney was discouraged. He prayed that the fire would not cease. When Finney arrived at his church for a prayer meeting, he opened the door to a powerful revelation of

God's glory. A heavenly light shone round about him much like with Paul on the Damascene Road and he fell to the ground.

His response is telling. Finney began to weep profusely as he shyly gazed into the great light at the unspeakable beauty of God. He explained later that he wept because he could realize that all things readily worship the Lord in the beauty of His Holiness except humanity. What a shame it was that any intelligent being neglected to completely give his- or herself to the flow of this excelling glory and love. What a thought!

Be encouraged as you consider this.

Process

"I the Lord search the heart and examine the mind, to reward a man according to his conduct, according to what his deeds deserve." —Jeremiah 17:10

Hear these chilling words: "The heart is deceitful above all things and beyond cure. Who can understand it?" (Jer. 7:9)

One theme that continues to reverberate in my spirit is that ACTING like a servant is not enough—one must BE a servant. This is to say, we must have a servant's heart. In order to gain this heart, we must undergo "spiritual heart surgery." I call this operation of God on the human heart "process."

I am enduring process even now. Process usually happens when God bestows a revelation that you can in no way live up to. Why? Because the human heart is deceitful, tricky, fickle, and wicked. When we see God right order, there is no way we can discipline ourselves to fit therein. But, God, by His wondrous grace, works a work in us inwardly and mysteriously makes us what He wants us to be. Now, this happens only as we are willing to endure process.

To be sure, I am not always willing. Actually, I seem to feel very unwilling more times than not. It is hard. But, God knows each of us intimately and will not give us more than we can bear.

May you find encouragement in these words.

Passion for Service

. . . Show me your face, let me hear your voice; for your voice is sweet and your face is lovely. —Song of Songs 2:14

I visited a dear man in the hospital once. His body was frail, his hearing poor and his eyes unfocused. I have never wept before after visiting anyone in the hospital, yet this time I pour out many tears. This man has lived his life with Jesus, and his glory shined on his face.

The Bible speaks about people being a reflection of God's glory. When this was written in Scripture, it was not just to wax poetic. The single-minded, simple faith of the examples in Scripture is rare and precious in these days. I got for a moment to see an example in this sick man.

The man could hardly eat to fill his stomach, but he was full of the Spirit. He was likewise filled with love for Jesus and exclamations of joy and praise often broke right in the middle of whatever he happened to be saying. He had a fire.

I am so glad I visited him. You never know how God will meet you in His blessed glory, except you may always know it will be during periods of service. He had a fire and fire cannot be taught, only caught. I caught a bit the that day and pray that you be encouraged to go catch some as well.

Power for Service

I am the vine; you are the branches. If a man remains in me and I in him, he will bear much fruit; apart from me you can do nothing. —John 15:5

Are you struggling with having meaningfulness in your life? Let me repeat the words of a great evangelist in the early 20th century: "God wants for us to be so completely dependent on Him that we will need to lean on nothing else." Nothing. This is a strong word. It is absolute. Christ does not leave any room for negotiation or compromise on this truth. There is nothing we can do apart from him.

Please do not be confused by this statement. The issue here is not whether or not we can accomplish significant things in life. We are not talking about the size or importance of a work. We are talking about service. We cannot fulfill any meaningful service without the purpose, power and presence of Christ.

Beloved, this point is more poignant in this generation than maybe ever before in history. In terms of world philosophy, we are entering in the first firmly post-Christian generation, where the "powers that be" are failing now to give even lip-service to Christ. People used to assume certain Christian ideas, values and perspectives, even if they were not faithful believers. Now more than ever, if God is going to be shown as real, it must be shown in our witness and our service.

Once before, Christ said, "and you shall receive power to be my witnesses." This is what we must lean on with all our hearts and souls. God wants to use you for meaningful service in this time. Seek him with all you've got; lean on Him and be encouraged—He will not let you down.

Take the Lead

Better a patient man than a warrior, a man who controls his temper than one who takes a city. —Proverbs 16:32

God has ordained for us to lead and disciple nations. Yet, before anyone can lead another, he must learn to lead himself. A great problem for the modern church is the lack of this kind of leadership.

We are often filled with complacency and fail to fulfill our potential. Why? Is it not that our time is filled with so much to do with so little time? Are we not overwhelmed sometimes with just "stuff?" We can only do so much and incorporating the kind of genuine devotion to God we yearn for seems difficult or near impossible.

Many of us hear the voice of the Father and some of us answer His call. But, the proverbial rubber hits the road when we move to accomplish His call. We must "know" and "do" God's will. If we know it and do it not, we sin. The discomfort we feel when we fail to step out on God's call is our inward knowing that we have sinned against God. Yet, God gives us victory over sin. (1 Cor. 10:13)

We must make major adjustments in our lives to follow after Christ. Following Christ will always bring you to a point where we have a crisis of belief. We will have to choose between the world and Christ. This is never done in a general sense; it is done as we walk the walk.

August 13

What is your hindrance? What "test" did you fail? Fear not. The chance will come again for you to stand for Christ and gain victory in your walk. And at that time, it will be an act of leading yourself—an act of your will—that will see you through.

Be encouraged.

A Pent Up Flood

From the west, men will fear the name of the Lord, and from the rising of the sun, they will revere his glory. For he will come like a pent-up flood that the breath of the Lord drives along. —Isaiah 59:19

This generation is a most distressingly godless generation. Not only does it lack the substance of godliness, it lacks even the form of godliness. What is more pitiable, beloved, is that many of us have become used to the state of things.

God's Word says, "Truth is nowhere to be found, and whoever shuns evil becomes a prey. The LORD looked and was displeased that there was no justice. He saw that there was no one, He was appalled that there was no one to intervene" (Isa. 59:15-16). Friends, our role is to intercede. God expects us to "cry aloud and spare not" (Isa. 58:1). "Come near to God and He will come near to you, " says the Lord, "Grieve, mourn and wail. Change your laughter to mourning and your joy to gloom" (Jas. 4:8-9).

God is waiting for us to seek after Him with ALL our hearts and ALL our souls. There is a small flame within each of our hearts begging at our attention. God's Spirit is gently calling. He will not force us out of our complacency at this time. He wants to know who really wants Him to come in like a flood. May your hearts be in sympathy with His. Let us clean our hands and purify our hearts so that, through and through, we are satisfied with nothing but Him. To this end, I encouraged you today.

Lean on God

*"Have faith in God," Jesus answered.
—Mark 11:22*

Lean on God. Put your whole weight on Him. Trust Him and do not doubt. God has been faithful in your life and has never failed to pull you through whatever situation you faced. Lean on Him and pour out your heart to Him.

Do not hold back anything in your heart. Take Him at His Word that He will give you the desires of your heart. Even when you desires are not godly, by opening them up to Him, you allow for the Spirit to shape and form them into what they should be.

Do not settle for anything less than what God has for you. His promises are rich toward you. His blessings are stored up as if in rain clouds bursting to pour forth. Yet, they will not come without our complete leaning on Him in prayer. God knows what you need and has stored these things up. Stop trying to work things out yourself, even in the little things, and trust in the Lord. Trust Him!

Can you say you love God dearly? Is there a great and flowing affection at the mention of His Name? Is there power in your confession of Him? Passion follows romance. Our spiritual affections depend on our spiritual experiences. God wants to love us in ways we can see, but waits for us to put our full weight on Him. Have faith in God and be encouraged.

The Blessings of Brokenness

The sacrifices of God are a broken spirit;
a broken and contrite heart, O God, you
will not despise. —Psalm 51:17

God will draw near to you to the degree of your brokenness. Many people are blessed. Both the just and the unjust receive favor to some degree. But, God reserves the blessing of His nearness for those with a broken spirit and a contrite heart.

Brokenness is not something quickly acquired. It takes faith and perseverence to develop it. The Bible teaches that when your faith is tested, make it your business to count it as a good thing ("count it all joy"). (Jas. 1:2-3) Tested faith produces brokenness and intimacy with God.

Stop complaining, beloved. God has not left you. In this world, you will suffer and go through. This is not optional and there is nothing to be done about it. We must learn to be broken and be willing to learn from what we go through. This may sound like a tall order—it is not. It is simple truth. Be encouraged.

Peace That Passes Understanding

And the peace of God, which transcends all understanding, will guard your hearts and your minds in Christ Jesus.
—Philippians 4:7

There is a difference between worldly peace and the peace that God gives. The world's peace is a pause between conflicts. God's peace prevails even when conflicts rage. God's peace is the only worthy peace. The world's comes and goes too often and as it pleases, if you will, without controls.

The Bible says, "Seek peace and pursue it" (Ps. 34:14). Do not be fooled by the notion that you have peace if and when you do not have GOD's peace. God promises to all who love Him that they may walk in divine peace. (Rom. 5:1; 14:17) If you are missing the bliss of peace—the intimacy with and acceptance from God our Father—I charge you to take hold of it in prayer! This blessing is yours by the firm promise of Scripture!

I desire so earnestly that you, my dear friends, would have all that God has prepared for you. No longer settle for less! If you must, find a quiet, lonely place so that you can truly wrestle with God and pour out your heart. Grab hold to Him in prayer and declare with a boldness afforded by the Cross that you "will not let You go until You bless me!" You will be in for a ride, God will shape and reshape your heart, but HE WILL ANSWER. I declare He will! Be encouraged.

Making Things Right

Settle matters quickly with your adversary ....
—Matthew 5:25

God is able and willing to lift you out of every mess, no matter how deep it may be. Yet, He will not allow you to escape a good measure of the consequences in the process. Unfortunately, sometimes we allow this to deter us from trusting in the Lord for our deliverance.

Do you really think you can fix your problem better than God? Many of us try to circumvent the pressure or humiliation that could occur when we become vulnerable and lay ourselves at God's feet. I know that I have in the past. Yet, when we try to cover up our "mess ups" or avoid the consequences, dear friends, we hurt ourselves all the more and put ourselves in deeper trouble.

Face up to consequences, whenever they present themselves. Deal with your unfinished business with urgency and do not delay. If you have it in your ability, pay your debt now. Jesus sees our natural tendency to flinch at God disciplining, but boldly called us to face up to things and make thing right. To this end, my friends, be encouraged.

Boldly in Prayer

Let us then approach the throne of grace with confidence, so that we may receive mercy and find grace to help us in our time of need. —Hebrews 4:16

What kind of boldness is needed to acquire answered prayer? There are prayers that we may assume God MIGHT answer. There are prayers that we WILL ourselves to believe God will answer. But, we may only have true confidence in prayers that we can pray with true boldness.

God expects us to approach Him with boldness, as a child to a parent. One should not presume to come to God with the boldness of a lion, per se. Our power with God is not in our ferocity or through bargaining power. Yet, much like a child has pull on the heart of a doting parent, we do have power with God and can boldly impress upon Him our requests. This kind of boldness comes out of a pure relationship.

Is your relationship with the Lord pure? Do you have guilt, or even shame, plaguing your heart when you go to Him in prayer? Sometimes I do. But, I am quick to deal with the issues of my heart. For when I pray, I do not mean to rise from my knees until the assurance that God has heard me fills my heart. I need boldness to acquire this security, so whoever deserves an apology, whatever decision needs to be changed, whatever attitude I must reject or take on, I see to it that it is accomplished. I hope this helps on today.

Praying in the Spirit

But you, dear friends, build yourselves up in your most holy faith and pray in the Holy Spirit. —Jude 20

I am convinced there are few prayers worth much of anything that are prayed without the help of the Spirit. There is a prayer with the Holy Spirit and there is one without Him. No earnestness, fervency, persistence or consistency will do when the Spirit of Christ has not aided you. Indeed, as I understand Scripture, you cannot really pray in the name of Christ without the Spirit's enabling. (1 Cor. 12:1)

The Holy Spirit aids us in prayer in several ways. First, He helps us to know how to address God by revealing His mind on this or that. The Bible says with inward moans and groans, He directs us as we pray. At this time, He gives us the sense to halt our request because it is fleshly or outside His will. At another time, He brings out our real desires are and helps us sift through the lesser (and often deceptive) desires in our heart.

God's Spirit also adds fire and urgency to our crying out to the Father. He adds to our spiritual momentum and helps it to intensify. Take this example. A car can roll down a hill, but will quickly decelerate when the slope changes. It needs more power to keep up speed or accelerate. The Spirit gives us power for prayer.

E.M. Bounds was a great man of prayer in the late 1800s and wrote hundreds of treasure-filled pages on the subject. In his discussion on "praying in the Spirit," he gave a wonderful image. When we pray, he suggests, we prepare and pour the stuff of our hearts. But, then the Spirit enflames this offering that it may rise into God's presence.

Let Him set fire to your heart and be encouraged.

The Secret of Intercession

But Moses sought the favor of the Lord his God. "O Lord," he said, "why should your anger burn against your people, whom you brought out of Egypt with great power and a mighty hand? —Exodus 32:11

Prayer for so many is such a mystery. So many have questions they do not even know how to ask. Our lack of understanding becomes particularly difficult when the object of our prayers has to do with a loved one or friend. How should we pray for one that has rejected God? What should we pray? When, if at all, should we stop praying? I have known many heart-wrenching stories.

Let me introduce this principle. When praying for another's salvation or deliverance, pray until or unless God tells you not to pray. Actually, God WANTS you to intercede; note the Scripture, ". . . and it displeased Him that there was no intercessor" (Isa. 59). I understand it like this: God seeks in His own initiative to reach the unsaved, but relents should they choose to squarely reject Him. He desires to continue in His pursuit, yet gives us the right to our choice. Yet, when we intercede, we give Him further cause to pursue.

Of course, God can choose to forgo this manner of dealing with us, but sets Himself to deal lovingly with us at all points. This principle is shown over and again throughout Scripture and, most notably, in the verse above. Therefore, let your heart pour out on behalf of your loved ones. Intercede on behalf of your friends. Pray and do not relent. As the Spirit aids you in prayer, you can firm up your hope that an answer is forthcoming.

ℐ Hatred of Sin

Let those who love the Lord hate evil, for
he guards the lives of his faithful ones and
delivers them from the hand of the wicked.
—Psalm 97:10

God wants us to hate sin. It is not enough to simply avoid it or to know that it is wrong. Much as we are to love God with all our hearts, we are to hate sin with all our hearts. We must hate it to its root.

We must make sure that we do not deal with sin in a superficial way. God will not hear the prayers for those that regard iniquity in their hearts. (Ps. 66:18) It is not enough to skate through a matter, resolving it only on the surface. The fact that you have entertained an evil motive in your heart is grievous to the Lord.

The Bible says, "Purify your hearts, you double-minded," (those that try to keep both the Lord and sin in their hearts) "grieve, mourn and wail." Know that your heart can never be revived and your prayers never fully answered, your walk with God will be severely hampered and your spiritual frustration greatly increased, unless you hate the evil you have regarded. Beloved, your blessings and spiritual treasures are in danger if you do not deal earnestly with the sin of your heart.

Your victory is in a broken spirit and a contrite heart. This, God will never despise. Be encouraged.

Hope For Healing

Naaman's servants went to him and said, "My father, if the prophet had told you to do some great thing, would you not have done it? How much more, then, when he tells you, 'Wash and be cleansed'!" —2 Kings 5:13

God does not really call us to do "great things." In truth, He calls us to "small things" so that He might do the great in us.

"Small things" are often a challenge for us. They involve taking care of details, being persistent, and often laying down our pride. "Small things" do not bring glory and honor to us, but to God when great things come out of them. This is the secret of divine favor. When we are faithful to do what He has asked, He will be faithful to do more than we dreamed.

We need great things to happen in the world today. The needs of human hearts are hurtfully deep. On one hand, we must be careful not to be overwhelmed. This will discourage us from doing anything. On the other hand, we must not deny ourselves the great crusade. We must focus on the small things, as instructed by God's Word, and look with great expectancy for the great things to come.

Forgiveness of Sin

'The Lord is slow to anger, abounding in love and forgiving sin and rebellion. Yet he does not leave the guilty unpunished; he punishes the children for the sin of the fathers to the third and fourth generation.'
—Numbers 14:18

Forgiveness is an amazing gift. It is when one has wronged you, yet you will persist in loving them. It deals with pain and hurt with a sense of justice, but without a hint of retaliation. It denies hatred's hold and makes trust possible for imperfect people. Forgiveness is divine. It is a trait of our Father.

Why does God forgive? It is hard to understand when faced squarely with this question. We all have a deep sense that we should get what we deserve in the end. We all are convicted that the guilty will be punished. But, God's heart is greater than this. He goes beyond being right to being good. When God forgives, it is beautiful and it often wins the wayward heart.

Forgiveness is powerful. It creates a righteousness greater than justice. Justice gives us our just due. Forgiveness excels to give us new life. Justice gives us recompense. Forgiveness gives us relationship. Justice gives us a sense of balance. Forgiveness gives us a sense of joy. It is a powerful gift and deserves more credit than what is often accorded it. Be encouraged.

The Great Cloud

These were all commended for their faith, yet none of them received what had been promised. God had planned something better for us so that only together with us would they be made perfect. —Hebrews 11:39-40

We are so blessed by the sacrifices of men and women of God who have gone before us. I am constantly reminded in my spirit that where I am and who I am has depended so heavily on the prayers and faithfulness of spiritual forebears. Especially when I mess up, I become more acutely aware of my unworthiness to walk in the honor that I do. I do not succeed by the grit of my own effort (God only knows the extent of this truth!). Whatever I have done, indeed, whatever any of us has done has been greatly helped by the faith of our spiritual mothers and fathers.

Consider this: when God gave our grandmothers or aunts or spiritual "godparents" vision, they often did not live to see it come to pass. We are now living the dreams of thousands of praying slaves, forlorn travelers, rugged pilgrims, and fallen warriors of faith. We do not deserve to be blessed. It is NOT our right. We lean, often unwittingly, on the mercy of God and his faithfulness to "establish the covenant He made with our fathers" (Deut. 8:28).

I encourage you today to give thanks. Know that so many of the blessings you have freely received cost so very much. Never forget those who have gone before. Never forget the great company, who are led by our Lord himself, that paid the price of faith to see to it that we might have the benefit of it. Blessings.

World Evangelism

". . . and you will be my witnesses in Jerusalem, and in all Judea and Samaria, and to the ends of the earth." —Acts 1:8

Have you thrown yourself into service to the Lord? Is your heart captured with passion for His causes? Many cannot say this because their vision is too small.

Evangelism starts in our own homes and outside on our own doorsteps, but its goal is the whole world. There is no greater sense of purpose when we see ourselves a part of a movement to change the world.

We must see the saving of souls in the context of reaching the world. Do not simply think about your church or your fellowship. Let your imagination wrap itself around reaching the world. Think differently and be encouraged.

Never Slothful in Business

Be . . . not slothful in business. —Romans 12:11

We live in a debt-driven world. So much we get involved with in our culture requires us to get in over our head. It can be so difficult to maximize the moment and avoid the unimportant. Overcommitment or being overworked often causes us to "drop the ball" on some important matters. Then, we must clean up the mess we have made and this often takes time and energy. Sometimes it seems like we will never get ahead.

God has an answer to our "busyness blues." He instructs us to be diligent and focused in our work. He wants us to minimize being reactive and to maximize being proactive with our time and energy. I call this getting on the offense.

In my favorite sport, football, you have offensive and defensive squads as a part of the team. The role of the defense is to get the team back on offense. There will always be defensive times, but we must remain focused on getting back on offense.

On the offense, we call the shots. We control the tempo of the game. We determine how things flow. Sometimes we will find ourselves overwhelmed, but we must push ourselves to get back on top of things as quickly as possible. Even when it seems impossible, YOU CAN DO IT.

Be encouraged.

Spiritual Life

..for the letter kills, but the Spirit gives life.
—2 Corinthians 3:6

Our prayer life is our spiritual life. We have no spiritual life without a prayer life. We receive "life"—this is to say power for living abundantly—from God through prayer.

The Christian life is about leaning and receiving. Leaning and receiving from God takes not only disciplined action, but a proper disposition. A vibrant prayer life does not come through simply having regular devotions or by praying a certain number of times a day. A vibrancy in prayer comes from an inward thrust to receive from God no matter what.

Take note of these words: "when you heart condemns you, God is greater than you heart" (1 John 3:20). Let nothing stop you from pressing into God and receive the grace you need at the time of need. He will answer if you seek Him with all your heart.

Be encouraged.

Righteousness, Peace, and Joy

For the kingdom of God is not a matter of eating and drinking, but of righteousness, peace and joy in the Holy Spirit. — Romans 14:17

We claim power in our Christian walk by grasping hold of God's great promises. (2 Pet. 1:4) One great promise is that all who truly live for the kingdom, God has granted them a victorious life consisting of righteousness, peace and joy.

The subject of righteousness deals with being in right order with God. This right order is founded on morality, but has further dimensions. As we have relationship with God, we must recognize His holiness and glory. Thus, we must do what is right AND live to give our best to him. For those who "seek first the kingdom" (Matt. 6:33), God gives grace to do this.

Peace is a state of mind. God promises a peace that is beyond understanding. (Phil. 4:7) This is to say, God gives us peace even in situations we cannot understand. God grants us peace through faith in Christ (Rom. 5:1) and, as we trust in him, we can know that "goodness and mercy will follow us all the days of our lives."

Joy is the product of the righteousness and peace we experience. It is the product, even more specifically, of answered prayer. When we walk in order with God and experience His peace through Christ, the end result is a rich relationship. We share intimately with God and God hears and answers our prayers. Jesus said that this was his source of joy and that he wanted us to have it. (John 15:11; 16:24)

These "great and precious promises" give us access into divine power for living. God wants you to live victoriously and to share that victory with others.

Be encouraged.

Stop Putting Things Off

He said to another man, "Follow me." But the man replied, "Lord, first let me go and bury my father." —Luke 9:59

There is oftentimes very little difference between a busy person and a person who puts off work. The "busy lives" that we face in this generation have created a culture of procrastination.

It is easy for us to excuse ourselves of this subtle sin of putting things off. We tell ourselves: "I have time," or "I'm not feeling this right now." Some of us relish the pressure, anxiety and consequential excitement of waiting until the last minute and rushing to the finish line. "Just so long as it gets done," we tell ourselves.

Procrastination replaces what is really important with what is not really important. It depends on trusting in shadows and favorable winds—we depend on time that God has not given us and has never promised. We presume upon God! The Bible says, "Do not boast about tomorrow, for you do not know what a day may bring forth" (Prov. 27:1).

We do have victory over procrastination. It is our sweet benefit as recipients of God's wonderful grace in Christ. Our victory begins with confessing procrastination as a sin. We often excuse it as a problem or a challenge or even a game. It is a sin. The wonderful thing about this, though, is that Christ died for our sins and though the Holy Spirit gives us power over sin. (Rom. 8:13)

I encourage you today, "put to death the misdeeds of the body" by the mighty power of the Holy Spirit at work within you and live your life for what is truly important.

Yes, God Loves You

. . . And I pray that you, being rooted and established in love, may have power . . . to know this love that surpasses knowledge— that you may be filled to the measure of all the fullness of God. —Ephesians 3:17-19

God has loved you enough to give you victory in Jesus, our Lord. We can easily miss this fact as we are driven through the rush of the day. We inwardly and constantly need the affirmations of God's love and He gives it freely. We, however, must be poised to receive it.

It does not take much to recognize God's love. We have memories of awesome ways He has blessed our lives from time to time. But, I encourage you today to take notice of the little things God does every day.

Some of these "little things" happen quite regularly (e.g., you wake up; you get well; you breathe). Others are special in the sense that we do not expect them—for instance, the song that really ministers to your heart comes on the radio at the right time; something in what someone says really helps you; you look for one thing only to find something else you really needed.

We all must learn the art of noticing the little details in God's handiwork. If you take time to look, you will see how intricate and ornamented they are. They have ruffles, a curves and points and color that are all set to dazzle you. Look, my friends. Be dazzled and be encouraged.

Issues of the Heart

The Lord your God is testing you to find out whether you love him with all your heart and with all your soul.
—Deuteronomy 13:3

What we do for God must always be with all our heart. We should do nothing for Him that we do not do from the heart. If you should find this difficult, know it is because you suffer from heart trouble.

Our hearts can either be tender or hard. The harder our hearts, the less the Lord can use us. There are many symptoms of this kind of heart trouble, but we may know we have a hard heart when we insist God give us our own way concerning this or that.

God wants to give you a tender heart. Hear His words: "I will give you a new heart and put a new spirit in you" (Ezek. 36:26). He does this often through putting you through a test. He will not put more on your than you can bear, but He will cause what is in you to come out. Sometimes this happens quickly; other times, it take a long time. But, do not fear if things are hard or look bad for you. God's loves you and has your best interests in mind. He will surely see you through. Be encouraged.

With All My Heart

I seek you with all my heart; do not let me stray from your commands. —Psalm 119:10

There is always a way back to doing what is right. You can always find your way back to the commands of God.

With earnestness it is written, "Commit your ways to the Lord." God desires not only to direct the general principles of your life, but to build character within you. God wants to show you what to do and how to be.

As you seek God with all our hearts, He will pour into you His character. You will begin to know intuitively how and how not to respond to things. You will have a greater, more blessed agreement with God's Word. You will feel stronger.

Do not give up when you have tried and failed in your life. Seek even harder. Right will come to you as you seek the Lord. Be encouraged.

A Broken Heart

Scorn has broken my heart and has left me helpless; I looked for sympathy, but there was none, for comforters, but I found none. —Psalm 69:20

Have you ever had a broken heart? It is hard to get over a broken heart. Things get cloudy. You lose touch with any sense of meaningful cause. "Helpless" is a good word to fit your feelings.

There is a difference between a broken heart and a wounded heart. Brokenness bespeaks completion, destitution, finality. A wounded heart can heal. There is a lesson that can be learned. But a broken heart is helpless—it is not a matter that it does not see its way out, it just does not matter anymore.

Dear friends, do not give up hope. It is not a matter of what you can do having a broken heart, it is what you do with it. Take your broken pieces to the Lord. Declare every sharp edge and detail every fragment as your prayer to the Lord. Pray not because of your broken heart (and by nature you will not); draw near through it and let the desperation of a muffled desire for God be the fire that sends your prayer to heaven.

The Spirit never leaves the broken heart. He hovers there. He confirms God's presence and His affirmation of you even when it is hard to care.

Be encouraged.

A Wounded Heart

*For I am poor and needy, and my heart is
wounded within me. —Psalm 109:22*

The Psalmist spoke a great deal about his own personal woundedness. It is to his credit and our benefit, lest we think we are alone when our hearts are wounded. It might just be that we will spend much of our lives enduring hardship. But, the grace of God is in knowing that we are built to last.

Despite how pessimistic this may sound, there is great victory in life for those that would choose it. Life is about walking through valleys; not staying in them. It is about climbing mountain peaks; not just overcoming bumps in the road. When I was a child, I decided it was better to be wounded "on purpose"—because I followed after purpose— than to be hurt without a cause.

Even now in these days, my heart does not always rush with passion for righteousness and for God. In times like these, I have realized that I just have to make up my mind what I want. Having done this, I get a new passion; one to break the malaise and grasp hold of Him who has gotten a hold of me. This takes guts, but this is what it means to love Him with all your heart.

Be encouraged.

Purity in Heart

Come near to God and he will come near to you. Wash your hands, you sinners, and purify your hearts, you double-minded.
—James 4:8

"Singularly God." This must be the cry of our hearts if we are to truly draw nigh unto Him. We draw near, not as if we can really reach Him in our own efforts, but as a gesture that we want Him and only Him. Can you hear the cry? Is your heart united behind this call to the Lover of Souls?

Do not become frustrated, beloved, if you find that you want to have this cry from your heart, but you do not have it completely. This is actually a sign of God's grace and the work of the Spirit in your life. I am learning what Watchman Nee said nearly 50 years ago: "my pursuing power comes from His drawing power." The Bible says the Spirit speaks to our spirits and creates a cry for our Father to draw near. (Rom. 8:15)

When the cry comes, we must set our hearts to cry it wholly. Notice in the above Scripture, it does not say, "God will purify . . . ." It tells us to purify. (Now we are not here talking about sanctification which is empowered solely by God's grace, but devotion which begins with God, but rests with our decisions.)

What do you want when you seek true devotion from someone else? Singular attention and persistence. Give the same to the Lord.

Be encouraged.

A Heart of Flesh

I will give them an undivided heart and put a new spirit in them; I will remove from them their heart of stone and give them a heart of flesh. —Ezekiel 11:19

We need a heart that can feel God. This is not a superficial, self-appeasing feeling. Rather, our heart needs to be constantly sensitive to the Spirit of God. We must have hearts that beat with the heartbeat of God!

God promises to give us this kind of heart. When we come to Him in devotion, He will do the inward work. This is empowered solely by His grace, for "the heart is deceitful and wicked, who can know it" (Jer. 17:9)?

Know that as you seek Him with all your heart, He will do the work in you to make you more sensitive to Him. He will give you the sensitivity and the wonderful joy of knowing His heart. He will open His mind to you. Seek Him, for there are treasures untold that He has for those that do. Be encouraged.

A Test of Character

Not only so, but we also rejoice in our sufferings, because we know that suffering produces perseverance; perseverance, character; and character, hope. —Romans 5:3-4

Growth in the Lord is a most rewarding experience. The Bible says that gaining this kind of growth is "more precious than rubies and more costly than gold" (Prov. 3:14-15). Growth in the Lord is growth in wisdom and character and bears eternal consequence.

This is why Paul states unequivocally, "the present sufferings of this day are not even worthy to be compared to the glory that shall be seen within us." This "glory with us" is the glory of character. And such a glory and treasure does not come casually.

Consider your ways. Can you today say that your are not the same person you were a year ago? Think on your life. How is it that you have come to grow? You have to "go through to get to" richness in virtue. Know that what you are dealing with now or what you will soon face will ultimately work to build in you an even greater weight of glory. Be encouraged.

Mettle

He will sit as a refiner and purifier of silver...
—Malachi 3:3

"Refine me, Lord!" Should this not be the cry of our souls? Many of us often spend too much time and concentration bemoaning our struggles. Pain is an inescapable part of life. We *will* fall, we *will* fail. Times will come when hope will be hard to have. But, we have a choice to struggle "in" or struggle "through."

The Scriptures call us to count it joy when tests come into our lives. God does not call us to be gluttons for punishment or lovers of pain. When He says, "count it joy," He means for us to understand the baseness of trials, but look past them to the glories that will be birthed out of them.

God says to us, "I see you." He is not distant from our sufferings. He is not indifferent concerning our confusions. He does not turn His face at our failure at trying. He sees us and whether in good or bad times, He means to refine us that our truest value may shine forth.

Seek this and do not shun it. Your life will be more precious for it. Be encouraged.

Standing a Change

For God said, "If they face war, they might change their minds and return to Egypt."
—*Exodus 13:17*

People with true mettle and who know their spiritual worth are willing to stand change. I have greatly admired the stories and testimonies I have heard about saints of the distant or not-so-distant past who made a difference in their generation. These men and women had a character and greatness which enabled them to pour out their inner treasure in their time. (2 Cor. 4:7)

The people who have grabbed the world's attention for God, have been those most willing to embrace life's trials. Like a warrior in mortal combat—like a mother rushing to her helpless child—like an adventuresome child experiencing a new world—like a frightened animal trapped in a corner—these noble hearts threw themselves into the unknown and weathered every storm. Complaining was done, but not often. Depression emerged, but not victoriously. Some thought to turn back, but not long and not without soon remembering that "this is what it takes."

Too many of us too many times cry over spilled milk. Times will bring us things to cry about; but, beloved, let us step back enough to see whether what we are dealing with is really a struggle against circumstances or with our deep-set desire to have our own way. There is no room in the kingdom for the latter—the battle's too real and the stakes too high.

Stand tall and be encouraged.

Spirit of Excellence

But I press on to take hold of that for which Christ Jesus took hold of me.
—Philippians 3:12

There are two states in which a person can live. The Bible says, "For he has rescued us from the dominion of darkness and brought us into the kingdom of the Son he loves" (Col 1:13). When we are saved, we are translated from living in the confusion of fleshly passions to living in the spirit of excellence.

Excellence is a spirit. It is not simply "doing everything right" or "doing all things well." These are the result of excellence, but its roots lie deeper. Its essence is in the determination not to accept less than what is best. The spirit of excellence is the drive, even when we fail short sometimes, to have ALL that God has for us in His great promises.

When God saved us, He placed in us a spirit of excellence. He revived within us His diminished image and gave us a drive to seek after His greatness and glory. This accounts for one's unsettledness when spiritually stagnant on one hand, and one's earnestness in prayer on the other. This is "what's got a hold of you" and what you are inwardly pressed to "catch hold of."

I encourage you today to walk in such a spirit and never to settle for less.

Healing Hope

The moon will shine like the sun, and the sunlight will be seven times brighter, like the light of seven full days, when the Lord binds up the bruises of his people . . .
—Isaiah 30:26

During the time of the 9/11 tragedy, I saw a man on television with his eyes wide open, his body set slouched on a silted sidewalk and with a hand to his mouth. No tears. No sobbing. The shock of the attack still loomed over him. I wonder what the sun looked like to him at that moment.

Terror claims our innocence and leaves us with eyes wide open. We simply will never see things the same way again. What do we do in the face of such horror? I take my cue from our dear Christian brothers and sisters in their countries facing persecution for their faith. These men and women, like the Master, are of "sorrows and acquainted with grief." I will put my trust in the Healer of broken hearts.

The sun does not shine today like it did before. It is not that the sun has changed; it is because the violation of our hearts veils our eyes. But, the Lord will arise with healing in His wings and we will see the light like we have never seen it before. With eyes wide open, look for this day and be encouraged.

A Word from the Lord

My eyes fail from weeping, I am in torment within, my heart is poured out on the ground because my people are destroyed, because children and infants faint in the streets of the city. —Lamentations 2:11

Grief is stupefying. In the face of senseless tragedy and inestimable evil, "the chief men refrained from speaking and covered their mouths with their hands" (Job 29:9). Who can speak in a time like this? What can be said? Who's words would have meaning?

There is a word from the Lord. "The Word became flesh and made his dwelling among us" (John 1:14). God does not just love us from a distance. He sent His eternal Son to dwell with us and to know us—even our pain. Jesus hurt. Jesus struggled in prayer. Jesus wept and indeed weeps today from eternity.

Jesus died a horrible and tragic death. Yet by it, he showed and proved God's heart of love for us. Even more wonderfully, in his sacrifice He provided us salvation from the lurking evil within us all that unchecked always leads to the unthinkable. His salvation is wonderful! Thank God for His Word to us!

Be encouraged.

Living By the Spirit

So I say, live by the Spirit, and you will not gratify the desires of the sinful nature.
—Galatians 5:16

God has given us tremendous aid by which we can live a distinguished and blessed life. This aid is supernatural and thereby gives us strength beyond strength to face the issues of life. God did not simply call us to walk according to the right way, but blessed us that we might be inwardly motivated to do righteously. This aid comes in and by the Holy Spirit.

The Holy Spirit not only leads us in our journey on God's pathway, He aids us and gives us strength to endure. The life that we must live requires this assistance. The evil of these times makes it clear that we will need divine assistance to live and to make a difference.

It has been a fact that so many of us who bear the honored title "Christian" have done so with complacency. I challenge and charge you now to throw off your hesitations and distractions, beloved, and seek God for the empowered life He has made ready for you. Ask for the Spirit to fill you and be obedience to His voice. Let us all encourage one another in this way.

Inspiration

Then the Spirit of the Lord came upon Gideon, and he blew a trumpet, summoning the Abiezrites to follow him. —Judges 6:34

The power of leadership is inspiration. To be truly inspired is to be Spirit-filled and Spirit-led with regards to a purpose. No one is Spirit-filled to "do nothing." Inspiration comes as a result of focus and commitment to a cause. But, when it comes, it empowers you to lead.

People long to be inspired. They long to be more than what they are. This is a side-effect of sin, for sin makes us "fall short of the glory of God"—that is, the glory for which and in which we were created. When you grasp firmly to purpose with commitment and do what it takes to ready yourself for it, God's Spirit will fill you and you will inspire others.

We make a difference in the world by making a difference in ourselves. Think on this and be encouraged.

Mature Servant Leadership

Therefore be as shrewd as snakes and as innocent as doves. —Matthew 10:16

A good leader is a servant and a good servant is a leader. Leadership and servanthood are two qualities that, by necessity, go hand in hand. God will not put the burden of true leadership on haughty shoulders. Nor can God depend on the service of those that do not lead themselves. We must build a maturity in Christ that involves tough minds and tender hearts.

In Proverbs it says one of the three things that disrupts the foundation of things is "a servant who becomes king" (Prov. 30:22). This is because the servant, in this case, is not prepared to be a leader. Yet, in much of the body of Christ, this is precisely what has happened. We have established leadership that has not matured in Christ-like character.

God is moving to change all this. He is raising up mature saints whose lives will be founded on wisdom and character. This is the leadership for the 21st century so many have been talking about. We are witnessing a switch. While once—for many, many years—the church was founded upon institutions and structures, it will soon rest squarely on the shoulders of mature saints.

Are you ready? Can God use you as a servant and a leader? Let God have His way in your life and understand that what He is taking you through is for a great purpose. Give up complaining and embrace the challenge. You're the leader God's been looking for. Be encouraged.

God Takes Sin Seriously

"'When anyone is guilty in any of these ways, he must confess in what way he has sinned and, as a penalty for the sin he has committed, he must bring to the Lord a female lamb or goat from the flock as a sin offering; and the priest shall make atonement for him for his sin." —Leviticus 5:5-6

God takes sin seriously. The book of Leviticus makes this very clear to us.

According to the Word, when a person sinned, a spotless and innocent lamb was taken and the person was charged to "lay hands" upon it. In this laying of hands was the transference of sin from the sinner to the sacrifice. Yet, implicit in this transference was to be a sympathy for the lamb on behalf of the sinner's heart. The sinner needed to "look" at the innocent creature that was going to die for him and experience the overwhelming weight of his sin. The wage of sin is death and he would have to witness the poor creature's death on his behalf and for his sin.

God reminded me of how this system of sacrifice eventually became odious to Him. After a point, He refused the offerings of His people. (Isa. 1:11-14) Why did He reject the system He had set up and given to humanity? The people took it for granted and they cared not for the lamb that was slain.

We all have a Lamb that was slain. Every time we

sin, we chalk it up to Him. Our willfulness, our shamefulness, our anger, our rejection of God's instructions and the direction of the Spirit, our unforgiveness, our lust for life and people and things, our neglectfulness, our lack of passion all counts against us but is chalked up to our Lamb. God forgive me for the times I have taken this for granted.

Look at the Lamb, care and be encouraged.

Learning through Serving

Whatever you have learned or received or heard from me, or seen in me—put it into practice. —Philippians 4:9

The best way to learn and build strong Christian character is through serving. Some of the most important life lessons are learned at the nursing home, the soup kitchen, the jail/prison, the hospital, the schools and on the streets. We learn of Christ best when we emulate him and serve others. The act of service is the classroom and the Spirit of Christ teaches us as we work along.

I encourage you today to think of where you can serve. You may not be able to spend a lot of time and change the world, but maybe you can change a little in yourself. Be encouraged.

Spirit Commitment

Into your hands I commit my spirit;
redeem me, O Lord, the God of truth.
—Psalm 31:5

So much of life is based on what you believe. Do you believe the truth or lies? Your life and joy and peace is based so much on whether you trust God's Word or your perception of your circumstances.

I know the seeming difficulty of trusting God's Word. Satan's barrage of lies can be very convincing at times. But, we must test our perception and conclusions. Does what we believe line up with God's Word.

God's Word says, ". . . I know the plans I have for you . . . plans to prosper you and not to harm you, plans to give you hope and a future" (Jer. 29:11). It says, "In my alarm I said, 'I am cut off from your sight!' Yet you heard my cry for mercy when I called to you for help" (Ps. 31:22). Does what you believe line up with this? Is your life wrapped up in these truths?

Following God takes a spirit commitment. You must lay your thoughts and attitudes "into His hands." I know it seems like the hardest thing to do. But, your faith will be greatly rewarded.

Be encouraged.

Get Ready to Lead

The Lord will make you the head, not the tail. If you pay attention to the commands of the Lord your God that I give you this day and carefully follow them, you will always be at the top, never at the bottom.
—Deuteronomy 28:13

God's intention for His people has always been to lead. We are predestined and appointed to lead the nations. This is an awesome call and even daunting when we look how we are now. But, our calling is sure and the way is clear if we are willing to follow it.

God says that if we learn His purposes and hear His voice; if we walk with Him according to His Word and His Way; if we "pay attention" to His commands, we will be divinely placed in position to give leadership to the every segment of the world. This is to say, we will speak into households and social groups, businesses and the various institutions, governments and economies.

It is sometimes hard to imagine possessing this kind of influence. This is because so many of us suffer from prolonged immaturity. I am thankful for how the Lord has enabled me to grow, but I must admit, I feel a bit behind spiritually. Yet, I hear the call loud and clear: "We must get ready to lead."

May you accept this as a goal for your Christian

walk. Prepare yourself, not just for service in the church, but to impact the world. You are the leader God's been looking for. Be encouraged.

Stepping Out on Faith

..Then Peter got down out of the boat, walked on the water and came toward Jesus. —Matthew 14:29

Jesus will almost always be out on the waters of our lives. It will always take risk to follow him. Thus, we can only follow him if we are willing to take risks.

The problem for most of us is not taking risks—it is taking risks over and over again. It is difficult to take risks after we failed the first time. Is it worth it to try over and again to walk closely with Jesus?

I often face discouragement. What I am learning through this is that the walk of faith is going to bring me into scary situations. Sometimes I long for the safety and security of some boat. But, I have discovered something: life inside boats is not worth living. For me, only the life lived on faith is a life that really worth it. You too?

Be encouraged.

Always Faith

Then the disciples came to Jesus in private and asked, "Why couldn't we drive it out?" —Matthew 17:19

Faith is not something to pull out or put up at will. Every thought and action is to be lived out in faith. Faith should be as natural and regular as breathing.

You must learn to count on God. His hand in your life is to be a given. This was what the disciples needed to learn in the Scripture lesson above. Faith is not just a response to challenges or situations, it is the way of life.

Have you really lived? Have you stepped out to walk on water? Have you claimed the destiny God has called you to and put yourself in a position that trusting God is a necessity? There is more in God than you or I could dream, but it takes an "always faith" to claim it.

Be encouraged.

Seize the Day

This is the day the Lord has made; let us rejoice and be glad in it. —Psalm 118:24

This day your are living in belongs to God. He made it and set a plan for it. You live in it and it is a blessing. Yet, responsibility is also a part of the equation.

I awoke one morning after a rather late night up with my infant daughter. At first I did not know where I was when the alarm rang. Its ring somehow became a part of my dream and I simply got up and switched it off.

When I gained a bit more consciousness, I prayed the Lord to add 5 more minutes to His 24-hour day. I had not yet opened my eyes, but God opened my ears and spoke to me. God told me, "Take charge of the day, for it is your charge to keep."

The Bible says that there is a time for everything. God has appointed this time and our charge is to be disciplined and sensitive to the Spirit. By doing this, we can avoid using time for one thing to do something else.

Seize the day beloved. Every conversation is not essential. Every time our eyes want to shut is not necessarily time for sleep. Every time we want to rest is not a time to stop working. Sometimes when we want to work, it is time to spend with family—or with our Father. Be encouraged, beloved, and seize the day.

Taking Charge of Time

But when Amasa went to summon Judah, he took longer than the time the king had set for him. —2 Samuel 20:5

When I was in college, I knew a Ph.D. student who knew what could be done with fifteen minutes. Whenever she found that much time to spare, she filled it with something productive. She had prepared herself to do this.

I am resolved to better value the time our King has set for me. For me, this means using my transit time for prayers to the Lord, finding a "steal-away" at work to take in a Bible chapter and prayer or phone call, and cutting my talk time. This is to name a few. It also means, avoiding unnecessary distractions and preparing my work better.

God does not call us to be efficiency experts, but he does call us to be prompt and diligent. Let us be encouraged to realize the value of every moment.

Building Character

Therefore, since we have been justified through faith, we have peace with God through our Lord Jesus Christ. —Romans 5:1

When I returned home from four years of college, I was amazed to realize how different things were. I remarked to my mother, "it seems like everything has changed." She replied, "everything hasn't changed, you have."

Building character is about change. When we look at situations in life that we want to change, we must realize that *we* must change first. Often, our first impulse is to rush into something—buy a new house, end friendships, find a new job, go to a different church. Yet, not one of these "answers" provides for the true change that we need.

I pity the man who faces a challenge and cannot learn from it. I pity the woman who cannot grow through her trials. The Bible teaches us how to face tribulation and build character. By faith in Christ, we are afforded peace with God.

True peace is not an "absence of conflict." It is power granted through God's grace. It is supernatural and experienced as we lean on God's care for us. It takes this peace to hold us while our world is "topsy-turvy."

If you want real, lasting and meaningful change,

you must actively have faith in God and endure. You must not run. God will translate your tribulations to tests, then to triumphs (Rom. 8:28).

Beloved, be encouraged.

See the End

Do not be afraid of what you are about to suffer . . . . Be faithful, even to the point of death, and I will give you the crown of life.
—*Revelation 2:10*

I encourage you today to reflect on where God is taking you in your life. God has a plan for your life that has abundant, eternal significance. There are literally thousands of thousands that have not heard of Christ. There are nations that have no relevant witness of the kingdom. There are people in our lives and families whose lives are broken and wounded. God is raising you up in His kingdom to shoulder the ministry to the world.

I speak this in light of the trials so many of us are going through right now. If you are like me, you had more than one thought of simply giving up and doing something else. I want to encourage you today to see the end. Recognize that the trials you are going through are like boot camp training and those that patiently endure will be those that can be used significantly for the kingdom.

There is a faithfulness unto death required for all of us. Though we may not face such violent persecution, let us be more willing to step into the line of fire. I know we are used to the ease and regular blessings of our lives, but there are brothers and sisters suffering violence in other parts of the world for the sake of Christ. Shall we grasp our ease and turn our face from the truth? No. This is neither in your spirit nor mine.

There is so much at stake. Be strong and courageous. There is truly a land we must take for the kingdom of God. In this, my beloved friends, be encouraged.

Falling Short

For all have sinned and fall short of the glory of God. —Romans 3:23

What do you do when you fall short? It is supremely difficult when your hopes are high and everything falls down around you. But, it is impossible to deal with when you fail yourself. Be encouraged, beloved, for God is able to handle impossible situations.

I am sometimes plagued with the thought, "If I had only done this or that, I would be more prepared—more mature, more 'in place'." Maybe I would not be falling so short if I had done things right the first time. This thought is so painful because there is truth to it.

But, consider this word: "[God is] able to keep you from falling and to present you before his glorious presence without fault and with great joy" (Jude 1:24). You may have fallen short, but God has provision to keep you from falling ultimately. God gives us a clean break from our past and allows us to have a future free of its bondage.

God says, "I will repay you for the years the locusts have eaten" (Joel 2:25) The sins and mistakes of our past may have opened us up to loss, but God will help us through it all if we put our entire trust in Him. I encourage you today to trust Him.

The Truth is the Truth

Truth is nowhere to be found, and whoever shuns evil becomes a prey. The Lord looked and was displeased that there was no justice. —Isaiah 59:15

We cannot do what is right until we are willing to acknowledge what is right. This is the challenge of this generation. We are a generation so often blinded by our advancements and prosperity—particularly in western nations. We feel that if we can sufficiently cover things up, the peace and ease we enjoy will be uninterrupted.

Yet, two cries disturb our truest rest. There is the cry deep in our hearts for crisp truth. Then, there is the cry of our conscience. These two cries go together—more exactly, they are one in the same. God is crying out in our hearts for us to seek after the truth so that we can work to do what is right. The poverty, conflict, murder and war in the world are not happenstance. They stem from the condition of each and every one of our hearts. They stem from our wrong priorities and our bad motives. (Jas. 5:1-4) They stem from our standing for what is wrong or not standing at all. (Esth. 4:14)

The world that is perishing needs a Church that will be "the pillar of truth." (1 Tim. 3:15) Yet, how can we stand together and be this when we will not shoulder the truth in our own individual lives?

Help Somebody

God is not unjust; he will not forget your work and the love you have shown him as you have helped his people and continue to help them. —Hebrews 6:10

The Christian life is not complicated. It simply takes dedication and sacrifice. When we live out the hope that is in us, so many of the distractions in our lives dissipate. One of the great joys in Christian living is the opportunity to help others.

God will help you to help someone. Sometimes, when situations come our way, we do not know what to do. A moment's prayer can often be enough to birth some direction. You may not have exactly what is needed, but many times the answer is just a phone-call away.

Offering help is spiritually invigorating. It is a powerful way for Christ to live out his life through you. It helps put things into perspective and strengthens your faith. It sheds light on what is really important and opens your eyes to what life is really about.

I encourage you today to look around you. There is someone that needs your help and God has blessed you to give it.

Know Your Season

Remember your Creator in the days of your youth, before the days of trouble come and the years approach when you will say, "I find no pleasure in them"
—Ecclesiastes 12:1

God has made us so that we move from one season of life to another. Each season has blessings and trials in it. Each one has a set of lessons that must be learned before we successfully move to the next. Do you know your season?

The fact is, so many of us do not realize our seasons. There are children who feel impressed to act like adults and adults who try reverting to their childhood. There are souls wounded by the failures of past seasons; they were so busy trying to be what they were not, that they missed out on important lessons. Some of us are just plainly playing catch-up.

God's wonderful grace is available for those of us who feel like we are playing catch-up. In His grace and love for us, God allows for us to take a make-up test, if you will. Now, we must be aware of this wonderful opportunity when it comes. If you find yourself facing the same challenges over and again, realize that it may be more of a blessing than a curse. It may be your re-test. The whole point is: we must know the season God has us in and be ready to face up to the challenges when they come.

Be encouraged.

September 29

The Centrality of Faith

We continually remember before our God and Father your work produced by faith, your labor prompted by love, and your endurance inspired by hope in our Lord Jesus Christ. —1 Thessalonians 1:3

We must be diligent to fill up what is lacking in our faith. Truly our Christian growth is a lifelong process. Yet, there is a point of maturity we can reach in faith where we can all but overcome the many pitfalls preventing our growth.

Maybe too often people think of faith in terms of what we can get from God. Faith has many more dimensions than this. By faith, we see things as they are— we get a spiritual perspective. By faith, we see God for who He is and tremble with love and godly fear. Faith guards us from being troubled in our hearts. It causes us to live well and with righteousness. Faith produces good works.

When we do not do our best, there is a lack in our faith. When we ignore our conscience, it is because our faith has failed. Faith is not simply a tool in our Christian life. It is central.

Be encouraged to strengthen your faith.

Simple Things

Now that you have purified yourselves by obeying the truth so that you have sincere love for your brothers, love one another deeply, from the heart. —1 Pet 1:22

Not many things in God are too boggling and complicated, they are just awesome. Love is this way. Love is simple. It only becomes complicated when we manipulate it or lack the courage to face its requirements. Now is a time for us to turn back to basics and rediscover the simplicity of love.

In love, when you say you will do something, you do it. If you fail to do so, you take responsibility for it. When we love, we accept others though we do not approve of everything they do. By love, we seek another's benefit for the simple reason of helping them advance. With love, we take to heart the cries of others and, when we are inspired by love, we echo these cries to God.

Love is all the Bible says it is in 1 Corinthians 13. Love is not always what love does, but love strives for the best expression. Love is not as hard as our hearts often are. Like an eagle learning to fly, it can be hard to start but when it is begun it takes on a power of its own. Remember love and be encouraged.

What Can We Do?

When the foundations are being destroyed,
what can the righteous do? —Psalm 11:3

God has called many of us into some very difficult situations. The situations are difficult because of the ungodliness that exists there. The foundations of decency, honesty, integrity, and other righteous virtues are being destroyed. What can we do?

When our hands are tied, we must recognize that God's are not. "The LORD is in his holy temple; the LORD is on his heavenly throne. He observes the sons of men; his eyes examine them." (v. 4)

Know that God has put you where you are for a reason. You may feel helpless, but the Lord knows what He is doing. Trust in the Lord. Let go of your control and know that God uses you even when you do not realize it.

Keep your integrity and do what is right. God is faithful. Be encouraged.

The Power of Praise

So will I sing praise unto Thy Name for-
ever, that I may daily perform my vows.
—Psalm 61:8

There is something enabling about praise. We must remember that our individual spirits are the central and most important part of who we are. When we are depressed or weighed down spiritually, it is hard to work or play. When we are spiritually enabled, we are empowered in every way practical. We must learn God's plan to keep ourselves "spiritually energized."

King David faced many distressing situations. From attempts on his life and coups d'etat for his throne to family troubles and administrative struggles with his officials, David faced a lot of stress. The fact is, like most of us, David was bombarded with troubles along the way and often felt discouraged.

In each case, David would claim God as his "shelter" and "strong tower." But, just claiming this was not enough. He did not just profess God's protection; He sang praises unto God.

When we give praises, we are acknowledging that one has performed or done well. Continual praise is a call for more. In the same way, David both acknowledged God's good work in his life and actively praised God for it expecting, if you will, an encore!

If you are burdened in your spirit, confess God's provision and protection and praise him for what He has already done. Then you will see the Lord moving on your behalf.

Overcoming Guilt

Blessed is the man whose sin the Lord does not count against him and in whose spirit is no deceit. —Psalm 32:2

How do you get over it when you mess up? What do you do when you lose confidence in yourself?

God has made us all to be mature leaders, but we often abdicate this responsibility because we are afraid of making serious mistakes. I know when I make mistakes, the first thing I deal with is: "should I even be in leadership" and "can I handle the responsibility?" This used to knock me into a funk for weeks at a time.

I have now learned that mistakes, even serious ones, are a part of life. We must learn how to move past our past and stay focused on walking in the life of God. We do this by being honest in our hearts and trusting God.

How prideful of me to think because I messed up, everything important in my life is finished. How prideful of me to think that I will have an untainted, sinless life. Beloved, God has given us all that we have, including our lives, and He alone is the judge of things.

Be encouraged, beloved friends.

Authority and Power

When the crowd saw this, they were filled with awe; and they praised God, who had given such authority to men. —Matthew 9:8

It takes authority to wield great power. Power may bring great respect, but authority is knowing what to do with that respect.

The people's hearts are not moved by power. They are moved by authority. Anyone can wield power, but only a good leader can manage authority.

Power brings fear, but authority brings wonder. It is the beauty of a good leader, not the power, that wins hearts. Good leaders manage authority without being authoritarian. Learn the wonderful art of authority and be encouraged.

Using the Good Word

*I delight in your decrees; I will not neglect
your word. — Psalm 119:16*

Once we come to know God's Word intimately,
we are prepared to use it for the issues of our lives.
As we study the Word at one point or another, we
consequently refresh ourselves of things we have
read in other sections. It is like connecting with the
Word at one point connects us to the whole. Our
minds become trained to think of things in terms of
God's Word. It is at this point that we can use the
Word in our lives most effectively.

As issues come up in our lives, we need to be able
to respond from a Biblical mindset. Too often we
revert to old, unregenerated practices when things
happen. We respond with our own strength instead
of in the strength of the Lord. God wants us to use
His Word and apply it to the situations of our lives.
He calls us to be careful to use it: "Only be careful,
and watch yourselves closely so that you do not forget the things your eyes have seen or let them slip
from your heart as long as you live" (Deut. 4:9).

Sometimes the Holy Spirit will bring Scriptures to
your memory when situations occur. At other times,
you will be lead to look up themes and passages in
your Bible. Yet, if you do not value the Word enough
to study it regularly, you will often miss God's
promptings. I encourage you today, my friends, do

not neglect God's Word. Think about it: by its power the very heavens and earth were established . . .

Morning and Evening

It is good to praise the Lord and make music to your name, O Most High, to proclaim your love in the morning and your faithfulness at night . . . —Psalm 92:1-2

The Word of God is a field of treasure as it relates powerful lessons for our daily living. The closer we look and the more diligently we study it, it yields precious nuggets of wisdom and understanding.

Many of us have sought after the Lord, saying, "Teach me Your ways!" The beginning of learning life-lessons from God is developing a devotional life. A time of devotion is a time of sharing personal closeness with the Lord. The acts of devotion are prayers and praise, singing and contemplation of His goodness (that is, His works, His ways, and His will).

The Bible over and again instructs us to share with the Lord both morning and evening. In times of crisis, we should spend even more time with God. (See Ps. 55:17)

The Bible also informs us on what we should accomplish in these times. In the morning "proclaim God's love (lit. lovingkindness)" and in the evening "declare His faithfulness." We should spend our morning times preparing for our day with God, laying our day out before Him and depending on His loving guidance. ("He guides the humble in what is right and teaches them his way"—Ps. 25:9.)

At night, we are called to a time of reflection and thanksgiving. We should declare, indeed out of our mouths, how God has been faithful to us throughout the day. This practice will keep our closeness to God vibrant and alive.

Be encouraged.

Rivers

Do to them as you did to Midian, as you did to Sisera and Jabin at the river Kishon.
—Psalm 83:9

There are many rivers talked about in Scriptures. They flow throughout Biblical history both freely and powerfully. There is always much meaning whenever a river is mentioned.

Rivers are life-giving streams. From the Nile to the Euphrates; from the Indus in the east to the Mississippi in the west; rivers have provided for the greatest civilizations the world has known.

Rivers are memorials. They are moving monuments of victory and defeat, success and failure, new beginnings and tragic endings. At the Kishon, Deborah and Barak defeated the oppressing forces. Elijah, the prophet, judged the prophets of Baal at this same river ending a reign of doom for Israel. This river has a story to tell.

There are rivers of the soul—times of significant memory. Triumphs and tragedy have etched a pathway in our soul. They wind themselves through our personality and sometimes run deep enough to impact our character.

"There is a river that makes glad the city of God." There is a river that flows large and strong over all other rivers, setting and resetting paths. The river of God's Spirit is able to make the difference in your life.

Be encouraged.

Reconciliation

All this is from God, who reconciled us to himself through Christ and gave us the ministry of reconciliation. —2 Corinthians 5:18

Now is a time for reconciliation. This is our main ministry. (2 Cor. 5:19) No doubt, we are to bring lost souls, indeed, this entire lost world to God. But, we are also to be brought back to one another.

God reconciles friendships. A hurt from a close friend can do the greatest harm. Yet, His forgiveness of our sins against Him enables us to forgive deep hurts. God reconciles marriages. We are in a wonderful season when God is renewing marital relationships by helping us see that marriage is more about Him than us. God reconciles racial divides. When people find themselves in God, they can no longer be threatened by others who are different or even opposed to them.

God reconciles families. He causes fathers to turn to sons and sons to fathers. He causes mothers and daughters to listen to each other. He brings such a peace and security that siblings release their rivalry.

When we are reconciled to God, we can truly be reconciled to one another. His power supplies our deepest needs and makes us able to love. Be reconciled and be encouraged.

Taking the High Road

*And quarreling arose between Abram's
herdsmen and the herdsmen of Lot. The
Canaanites and Perizzites were also living
in the land at that time. —Genesis 13:7*

How do you handle conflict? Maybe the most
talked about Bible ethic regarding this is: "When
your brother strikes you on one cheek, turn to him
the other." But, how is this done?

My mother taught me when I was a boy to always
take the high road. She told me, "Do not let quarrel-
some people bring you down to 'their level'." This is
exampled in Scripture with the patriarch, Abraham.

When there arose a conflict between he and his
nephew, Lot, Abraham "took the high road" in the
following ways:

1) Abraham took initiative. He sought to diffuse the
   situation before it blew up. Try never to resolve
   situations in the heat of anger. Conflicts are
   resolved when we talk to each other and not at
   each other.
2) Abraham put the other first. He led Lot into
   choosing a viable solution for both of them. He
   took himself out of the way and, by doing so,
   "stood above" the conflict.
3) Abraham let love be his guide, not anger. He
   thought about how both parties could win. He did

not respond to the situation because he felt violated; rather, he worked toward the benefit of both sides.

4) It was understood that the enemy was near. A division between Abraham and Lot could give an opportunity for the enemy to come in and destroy them both. We must also understand that Satan is on the look-out "seeking who he may devour."

Be encouraged to take the high road, my friends. God bless.

Never Admit Defeat

My eyes have seen the defeat of my adversaries; my ears have heard the rout of my wicked foes. —Psalm 92:11

There is power is positive confession, but this principle has its weaknesses and limitations. Many of us have been disappointed because with everything in us we have tried to stay positive in a situation only for it to end miserably. Hearts broken from this experience are hard to mend.

How do we persevere through tough times when it seems like we are completely powerless? How do we avoid the notion that "there's nothing I can do to change it so I've just got to accept it?" Never, never, never admit defeat.

David the poet-warrior-king faced discouragement on most levels. It is not hard to show that at times he FELT like giving up on life. But, he encouraged himself in the Lord. He did NOT encourage himself with pithy confessions or positive thinking. He chased after God in prayer and through praise and worship. When he found Him, God lifted up his head.

Never, never, never admit defeat. If you have gone as far as you can go, go further anyway. Press into God's presence and He will show you defeat—not of you, but of your Enemy. Be encouraged.

In Line for Blessings

In vain you rise early and stay up late, toiling for food to eat– for he grants sleep to those he loves. —Psalm 127:2

Never in the Word does God denounce hard work. Yet, God wants us to understand that it is not hard work that brings His favor and blessings.

We often seek after blessings in this life through our own strength. We "rise early" and "stay up late" working the day through. What we must realize is that we are working in the curse. In the beginning, God cursed the ground for as a result of Adam's sin. The curse was one of hard labor for minimal results. In doing this, God wanted to teach a lesson.

Many of us are hard at work right now for minimal results. No matter how much money we earn, or how hard we work, we are just making it through. We save enough through several months for a nest egg or to pay off some long-term debt and the car breaks down, or we have to call a plumber, or we need repairs on the house—in short, something comes up.

This is what life is like when we do not trust and are not in order with God. We need to get in line for HIS blessings. The Bible says, "He grants sleep for those He loves." In other words, God will still be cutting deals while we are sleep. God does not want us to live by the curse, but by His blessings. Step into the blessings, step in line and, in all things, be encouraged.

Living God's Life

> *But these are written that you may believe that Jesus is the Christ, the Son of God, and that by believing you may have life in his name. —John 20:31*

The Christian life is all about living out God's life in ours. God sent His Son so that we may have life and wants us to have life in his name. We live God's life in Christ in two ways.

First, we live out God's life through surrendering completely and understanding that our life is no longer our own. This is not our life to live. "We were therefore buried with him through baptism into death in order that, just as Christ was raised from the dead through the glory of the Father, we too may live a new life" (Rom. 6:4). Paul also said, "For to me, to live is Christ . . . " (Phil. 1:21). In other words, "I endeavour to carry out Christ's life through mine and thereby allow him to live in the world through me."

The other way we live God's life is by connecting to His power. Peter says, "His divine power has given us everything we need for life and godliness through our knowledge of him who called us by his own glory and goodness. Through these he has given us his very great and precious promises, so that through them you may participate in the divine nature and escape the corruption in the world caused by evil desires" (2 Pet. 1:3-4).

God provides His promises through the Bible and our experiences that are in line with His Word. As we take hold of His great promises, we not only experience His "glory and goodness," they become a part of our lives. This way God "powers" a life turned to Him and available for His use.

Be encouraged.

Courage

> *"Rise up; this matter is in your hands. We will support you, so take courage and do it." —Ezra 10:4*

It takes courage to stand up and do what the Lord wills. The Christian walk is not for the squeamish. This reality may seem harsh, but its truth will make us free.

I have met many a soul that has made a personal confession of Christ. They had come with an earnestness to be saved and to have Christ change their life. Yet, in the long run, they ended up back where they had started. With their hope for change diminished, their last state is often worse than their first.

When we surrender to Christ, we take a step of faith. This is an act of courage. It takes courage to follow along a new path; it takes courage to walk in victory each day.

I want to encourage you today to walk boldly in what God has said. Be encouraged.

What God Can't Help

A generous man will prosper; he who refreshes others will himself be refreshed.
—Proverbs 11:25

God has an giving heart. He searches out our needs and knows the desires of our hearts. One cannot seriously read through the Bible without being stricken by His compassion and mercy and giving.

Sometimes we have the wrong idea about our Father. He is not holding back blessings until we earn them. He does not transact with us in any stoic or business-like manner. God is bursting to bless us, though He is careful not to give us what we cannot handle.

I am encountering God's giving heart afresh. As He is calling me to Himself, I am seeing myself and how much I have to learn in this area. The Bible says, "Your own soul is nourished when you are kind . . . " (Prov. 11:17, NLT) God is showing me that to truly experience His heart, I must surrender my heart to being a giver like Him.

When it comes to giving, God just cannot help Himself. It is not just something He does—it is His nature. May our nature be all the more like His. Be encouraged.

Happiness

"Come and share your master's happiness!'" —Matthew 25:21

There is a difference between the happiness the world brings and the happiness of God. The happiness of the world in ultimately meaningless. It does not satisfy. Only God's happiness is worth anything.

God's happiness is eternal as God is eternal. To taste it is to taste a thing most precious. It is unlike anything else. It is not about a high or a rush; God's happiness cannot be pit against other things because it makes everything else wonderful.

The most wonderful thing about the happiness of God is that it is not elusive. It remains so accessible. God calls us to it and offers it to us. You can have it now if you want it—but, it will change your life . . .

Be encouraged.

Where Are You?

But the Lord God called to the man, "Where are you?" —Genesis 3:9

When God calls to us, "where are you," it is not because He does not already know. Should sin enter our lives, our first thought is to hide. We multiply lies to cover our misdoing or retract from everyone to hide our shame. Yet, there is no place we can hide from God and there is nothing to blind His view of us. When He calls to us, "where are you," it is for our sake.

God always gives us a chance to come back to Him. How much better it is, when our thoughts turn back to God after doing wrong, to immediately confess and fall at His mercy. How much better it is to see His call as an act of grace and not judgment. Truly enough, the Lord chastens us when we sin; but, "the Lord chastens only those that He loves."

Be encouraged.

The Principle of Love

Now about brotherly love we do not need to write to you, for you yourselves have been taught by God to love each other.
—1Thessalonias 4:9

Love is about putting others first. It starts with something within us, but we must learn how to bring it out. In other words, God puts it in us that we must love, but we do not start off knowing how to love. We must learn this.

Learning how to love is a life-long process, yet we can gain some consistency and maturity in it. God is the teacher in this process and He teaches us how to love through the gentle promptings of His Holy Spirit. On our part, this process can be mostly trial and error. God prompts us and when we obey, we experience blessings; when we disobey, we are convicted and must confess the lesson in order to grow.

Be intentional about learning this lesson, beloved. Pay attention whenever God prompts you to do something that puts others first. Recognize when you succeed and confess when you fail. By this, God will strengthen your character and bring you into a new level of maturity.

May you be encouraged in God's Word this day.

Duty

*So you also, when you have done every-
thing you were told to do, should say, "We
are unworthy servants; we have only done
our duty." —Luke 17:10*

So much in service is done secretly with self-
interests in the background. We must be careful.
Service to the Lord and to others for his sake must
not be done this way.

One way we can defeat the urge to place self-
interest in our serving and giving is to recognize the
ways in which God blesses and gives to us. The
Scriptures say, "And he died for all, that those who
live should no longer live for themselves but for him
who died for them and was raised again." (2 Cor.
5:15)

We must constantly relinquish our rights to ourselves and confess our dependancy on Christ. We
must trust in his provision as we live with moderation, faithfulness and as good stewards of his blessings. We must offer thanks continually and grow in
our knowledge of God and His promises. When we
do these things, how can we but declare to the Lord
that "we are unworthy servants; we have only done
our duty."

Be encouraged.

Condition of the Soul

Find rest, O my soul, in God alone; my hope comes from him. —Psalm 62:5

What is the condition of your soul? In its most natural state, our soul is to be at rest. This is where it thrives and flourishes. Yet, for many of us, our souls are restless. I urge you, beloved, do not focus so on the urgent that you lose sight of what is really important!

Consider what the Word says. "Do not wear yourself out to get rich; have the wisdom to show restraint" (Prov. 23:4). Again, "Better to be a nobody and yet have a servant than pretend to be somebody and have no food" (Prov. 12:9). In another place, "Better a dry crust with peace and quiet than a house full of feasting, with strife" (Prov. 17:1).

We are driven in this world to strengthen our standing, expand our possessions, grow our wealth, fulfill our "desires," accomplish our ambition, etc., etc.. Yet, Jesus said, "There is only one thing needful . . ." (Luke 10:38-42). Do you know what it is? Are you focused on it?

Be encouraged.

Encouragement for the Day

*My purpose is that they may be encour-
aged in heart . . . —Colossians 2:2*

My dear friends, be encouraged to move into the great riches of purpose and blessing that God has for you.

No matter how deep you get in God, there is always more. Never settle for what you already have. Keep pushing and pressing into His presence. Do not settle for less. Let your heart be "spoiled" by constancy in His presence.

"I love you." This is God's word to you. Do not let your relationship with Him degrade into anything less than a love relationship. Be encouraged today.

Be encouraged.

Good Timing

. . . the wise heart will know the proper time and procedure. —Ecclesiastes 8:5

The old saying goes, "timing is everything." This bears great truth. It is important that we receive wisdom from God to do what we do better. Do not be settled as you see that the job is getting done. Work more diligently at improving yourself and your performance.

Know that your performance at work or in a special project is a witness to Christ. When you strive to do well, that speaks to your relationship with him. When you do not, that also speaks volumes about your faith.

Those that earnestly strive to do better, do so by learning timing and procedure. Is how you do things the more efficient way? Are you careless with you time, easily becoming distracted in chit-chat or computer card games? Do you find too much relief in idle chatter?

Let the world know that your life and your time is precious and they will see your wisdom. By this, you will bring more praise to our God than a thousand words of testimony. Be encouraged, my friends.

When God Blesses

I am a wall, . . . Thus I have become in his eyes like one bringing contentment. — *Song of Songs 8:10*

The blessings of the Lord are not earned. They come from His tremendous heart of love for us. And He has given us licence to move His heart. We move the heart of God when we keep ourselves for Him.

What does this mean, to "keep ourselves for Him?" We must keep our hearts and conscience pure. Do not open yourself up for derision and strife. Avoid and despise evil thinking. Be honest with yourself and refuse to be led by your deceptive heart. Treasure God's words and hide them in your heart.

If you will do these things, God's heart will be won and your life will be filled with so many blessings. It is wonderful to live knowing that my destiny is not in my own hands and that the blessings of God will continue to see me through. May you know this same joy.

Be encouraged.

Thankfulness and Maturity

Open for me the gates of righteousness; I will enter and give thanks to the Lord. —Psalm 118:19

The greatest principle and the foundation of maturity is love. The greatest aid to maintaining a loving attitude is true thankfulness.

Love focuses on others and rejects self. It is empowered by selflessness and striped of its power when we are self-centered. The greatest means of tearing down our self-focus and, as the Scripture says, "mortifying (killing) the deeds of the flesh," is cultivating a truly thankful attitude.

Practice noticing what people do around you and for you. Take time to think about it. Our busyness often robs us of our minds and good sense. Take time to stop and consider the ways God blesses you through people or circumstances. God will teach you so much when you practice listening, looking, noticing and being thankful.

Be encouraged.

Encourage Yourself

Why are you downcast, O my soul? Why so disturbed within me? Put your hope in God, for I will yet praise him, my Savior and my God. —Psalm 42:11

Sometimes you just have to preach to yourself. Character is the ability to lead yourself and God is working in you to have a strong character. While you go through whatever you do, know that through the grace of God it is in your power to be encouraged.

How do you see life? Do you trust that, come what may, you will be all right? Do you trust that God is in control and will not see you "out for the count?" You must believe and hope in God! He is faithful and wants deeply for you to know this about Him. The assurance that He gives us is the grace by which we can encourage ourselves.

If you are down today, tell yourself to get up. God has not left you. God will never leave you no matter how bad you mess up. He went through too much to bring you to Himself; He is not going to cast you away. Hope in GOD and "yet praise Him." Be encouraged.

In Christ

Greet Andronicus and Junias, my relatives who have been in prison with me. They are outstanding among the apostles, and they were in Christ before I was. —Romans 16:7

One of the most profound understandings God has poured out in me is what it means to be "in Christ." The New Testament is replete with this phrase. Paul uses it profusely, but never lightly. The life and energy of the Christian walk is wrapped up in it.

To be "in Christ" is a state of being. We enter into this state when we surrender our lives to him and his Holy Spirit unites us with other believers in his Name. For Paul, generally speaking, to be in Christ was to be in the Church. In fact, he pushes the image and understanding far enough to say that we, the Church, are Christ's Body.

What does Paul mean by this strange phrase? So many of us are used to hearing that we are the Body of Christ, or that we are "in Christ." What is the practical significance? As the Body of Christ, each of us who are in Christ are united to "fill his shoes" while he is away. This does not simply mean that we are to fulfill good works in the Name of Christ, though this is an awesome responsibility. We are to fulfill his life. By the Spirit of God we become partakers of his very life and living.

Beloved, if your are "in Christ" what you are going through in your life will without fail turn out for eternal glory. Your life is tied up with Jesus Christ and "God will work all things together for good." If you are suffering, know that it is not meaningless because God will not allow anything into your life that will not eventually pay eternal dividends. You are "in Christ." Your life is tied in him and his life is tied in you.

Be encouraged.

Courage in Christ

Be on your guard; stand firm in the faith; be men of courage; be strong. —1 Corinthians 16:13

Take courage in who you are in Christ. Never give up. Learn to "put on Christ" and walk in your destiny in his Name.

Do you know who you are? Many times we falter because we cannot appropriately answer this question. My wife and I encourage our infant daughter to learn who she is. We encourage her to reach out and touch things; we want her to experience things. We are also teaching her appropriate limits. She is learning the word "No," though we are very careful when we say it to her. Our prayer is that she will grow in confidence, understand right and wrong. Our hope is that she will learn her place in the world and stand firm in it.

We must learn our place in Christ. We can only learn it, as my daughter does, through reaching out, experiencing new things and learning from them. We may feel too old to do this, but this is not the case. Stretch out of your settled life and test out new dimensions in Christ. He will lead you and teach you and tell you "No" when its time.

Be encouraged.

Christian Maturity

But solid food is for the mature, who by constant use have trained themselves to distinguish good from evil. —Hebrews 5:14

Jesus calls us to Christian maturity. He is not interested in simple morality— that is, being as good as the next person—or simplistic faith. He wants us to walk with shoulders broad enough to carry out a good work for his Kingdom.

The early Church was founded on maturity. They did not have rigid rule books, dry policies and institutional structures. In fact, their claim to fame was that they did not need them! (Gal. 3:22-23) Instead, they had a spirit of maturity which led them in mutual respect, diligence, dependability and love.

We, like the early Church, must become mature enough to work effectively for God's kingdom. We can do this when we have a foundation in God's Word and gain a commitment to do things well in His sight.

May God Be With You.

Spiritual Conflict

Set your minds on things above, not on earthly things. —Colossians 3:2

Open spiritual conflict is on the rise. You may run into it and not know what it is. Many arguments you have, many conflicts you endure, many disappointments you face, often stem from deeper sources. You can try to understand the situation rationally, but you will not. The problem is not rational, it is spiritual. (Eph. 6:12)

We must develop a Biblical worldview. Many things that we face on a day to day basis are spiritual realities, not natural. You can only deal with spiritual things in a spiritual, Biblical way. The Word prescribes discernment and prayerfulness for times like these. (Matt. 16:21)

If you run up against roadblocks in you associations, be discerning. Satan would have you "worked up" and stress out. If you find yourself unusually unnerved, take your rightful authority over that situation by confessing God's peace and verbally rebuking the enemy. Seek a mature Christian and counsel with them about putting on the whole armor of God and walking in your authority.

There is no hiding the fact of spiritual conflict. It does not set well with what our culture generally believes on the surface. But, it is undoubtably real. The good news is, however, that "we are more than

conquerors through him who loved us" (Rom. 8:37).
Be encouraged.

Decisions

Then David called one of his men and said, "Go, strike him down!" So he struck him down, and he died. —2 Samuel 1:15

Every Christian is a leader and must know how to make life and death decisions. When the Church is filled with compromise, it is because Christians were found incapable of doing this.

The cause of the Kingdom calls for boldness. We must be bold to witness to the Name of Christ. We must take risks and exercise faith if we are to win lost souls to the Lord. If we would see great power of heaven in our lives and ministries, we must be able to make good choices and strong stands.

Every decision in Christ is not popular. The truth is not popular and is often assassinated in public culture. Yet, we must learn to follow after the Lord, no matter what the cost and trust that He will take care of all else.

Be encouraged.

Lights in Darkness

"You are the light of the world. A city on a hill cannot be hidden." —Matthew 5:14

On today, many are blindly—or, not-so-blindly—celebrating the pagan Celtic holiday of *Sahmian* (pronounced, "Sah-ween"). On this day, they dress as ghouls and goblins. Children go from house to house with the mischievous phrase, "trick or treat." For many, this day is a day of harmless fun and maybe even of sharing and community. Yet, underneath this benign facade is some dark truth about, statistically, one of the most dangerous days of the year.

What is our response? What should we do? We might be encouraged to know what the dynamic, Spirit-filled Celtic Church did. In the face of this dark day, when pagans dressed as witches and devils and practiced horrible sacrifices, the church sought to be a light in darkness. "All Saints Day," which was held in May, was moved to the time of this demon's festival and was celebrated as a show of the victory of Christ over the darkness.

Today is a day for saints of God to take over the territory of the darkness. I encourage you, let God use you to be a light in the darkness today and from now on.

All Saints Day

Therefore, since we are surrounded by such a great cloud of witnesses, let us throw off everything that hinders and the sin that so easily entangles, and let us run with perseverance the race marked out for us. —Hebrews 12:1

Remember those in prison as if you were their fellow prisoners, and those who are mistreated as if you yourselves were suffering.—Hebrews 13:3

It is important that as witnesses of Christ we understand our connection with those who have done well and gone before. We are not isolated in history. (I fear some of our rants about "tradition" have made some of us feel this way.) We have a great and mighty heritage of holiness to take part in and uphold.

I encourage you today to think on the life of that Christian person who greatly impacted you, whether personally or at a distance. Let their witness strengthen your passion for Christ and souls.

As we remember those that have gone before us, "the trophies of God's grace," let us also remember those who hold our great testimony amid strife and persecution. From Sudan to India to Ireland to China; Pakistan, Vietnam, and Sri Lanka; throughout the "10/40 Window," from North Africa to Iraq; everywhere men, women, boys and girls bear the marks of Christ on their bodies. Remember them today and pray "as if you yourselves were suffering." May we all be encouraged.

Be Filled with the Holy Spirit

Do not get drunk on wine, which leads to debauchery. Instead, be filled with the Spirit. —Ephesians 5:18

God has added a dimension to our lives through His blessed Holy Spirit. He promised a certain power when the Holy Spirit came upon us. (Acts 1:8) A certain unearthly quality can be ours through faith in His promise.

You do not have to go it alone. God has stored up power for you to face the challenges of life. If you are suffering, God will comfort you through His Holy Spirit. (John 14:26) If you are distressed, His Holy Spirit will lift your head. (Rom. 5:5) If you are worried, the Holy Spirit will give you courage through God's promises. (1 Cor. 2:12) Christ promised that he would not leave you as an orphan; He comes to you in the Holy Spirit.

Make it your constant endeavor to be filled with the Spirit. Do not be drunk with the wine of this world—with its trappings and lusts. Seek after God with your whole heart and you will find Him. He longs to fill you and make you full.

We Serve the King

How awesome is the Lord Most High, the great King over all the earth! —Psalm 47:2

Hallelujah! "God is the great King over all the earth!" He is awesome, full of excellence and excelling stateliness. He declares the end from the beginning and does not miss a detail. He has millions and millions of attendants seeing to the very finest point of His will. At the pronouncement of His Name, people will not stand as they do for a president or judge, but, "every knee will bow and every tongue confess!"

We serve a God who is a great King. He is not distant and aloof, but has a heart for every soul in His dominion. Lies, deceptions and perversities are His enemies, but they cannot stand in His presence. We may see that "truth is fallen in the streets" (Isa. 59:14); we may see hopelessness and destitution around us; but, God is a Living God and He has given us power to take His life and light into a darkened world!

We serve the King! He will resource us. He will direct us. He will use us and prepare us. He will go with us. He will go before us. And we will gain victory each day in His Name. Bless His Name, beloved. Bless His Name!

Reconciliation

. . . And he has committed to us the message of reconciliation. —2 Corinthians 5:19

The fact that God speaks to us is amazing. For some in this world, it is unbelievable. Yet, the central gem of the gospel is that God "makes room for us in His life." We can talk with Him and He talks to us.

God speaks by the Holy Spirit in two major ways: He speaks to us by His given Word, the Bible, and through an active, proceeding Word. (I Tim. 3:16,17; Matthew 4:4) Through the Bible, God gives our life a foundation of truth. We learn who He is, what He has done and what He wants for us in life. The Word of God is eternal, unchangeable, and undeniable.

Yet, God also speaks directly to us by the Holy Spirit through prayer, circumstances and godly counsel. He did not just leave a record and stand afar off as an "absentee father." He leads us and guides us personally. By His Spirit living inside us, He comforts and enlightens us. We have relationship with God through the work of Christ on the cross.

How amazing is the Father's grace! How wonderful is His love! How deep is His wisdom and counsel! Beloved, there is only one thing we really need—reconciliation with God. Once we have that, everything else will follow. Be encouraged.

Prayer for Our Leaders

I urge, then, first of all, that requests, prayers, intercession and thanksgiving be made for everyone–for kings and all those in authority, that we may live peaceful and quiet lives in all godliness and holiness.
—1 Timothy 2:1-2

Scripture in many places calls us to seek after a climate in our land that will allow us to live "peaceably and quiet" with godliness and holiness. The leaders we have play a most important role in this and we must earnestly and consistently pray for them.

Proverbs says, "the heart of the king is in the hand of the Lord . . . He turns it whichever way He chooses." God is waiting for His people to pray and would do mighty works to influence our country if we would.

We must pray for their salvation and for them to recognize the Lord's fear and His righteousness. We should not simply politically support a person, and not consider their soul. Let us follow through with prayer.

Be encouraged.

The Truth

Therefore each of you must put off false-hood and speak truthfully to his neighbor, for we are all members of one body.
—Ephesians 4:25

There is a distinction between a lie and a deception. Lies are the broad range of attacks against the truth. Deception mixes a lie with the truth, taking away its power to make us free. It is kin to perversion which twists the truth, if only a little bit, for some defiling end.

The Adversary used deceptions when tempting Jesus. (Matt. 4:6) He quoted Scripture (the truth)—yet, out of context (the lie). He used it to weaken the foundation of the church after Pentecost (Acts 5:1-11). Ananias and Sapphira tried to finagle position and personal privilege using lying and intrigue. Jesus foretold that Satan would sow tares among God's wheat. Both John and Paul asserted that there are people among us that are not "of" us. (1 John 2:19; 2 Tim. 2:9; see also, Jude 4)

Deception is a tremendous challenge to the move of God, unity in the Body of Christ, and to our Christian walk. It is insidious. If you are being challenged today in your growth in Christ; if you lack boldness and freedom; if you desire greater closeness with our Father, then set your heart completely and solely on God's truth. Stop rationalizing your own way. A half commitment to God is simply not worth it. Trust Him completely, beloved. He wants to win your heart.

The King-Dominion

He is the image of the invisible God, the firstborn over all creation. For by him all things were created: things in heaven and on earth, visible and invisible, whether thrones or powers or rulers or authorities; all things were created by him and for him.
—Colossians 1:15-16

Hallelujah! Christ is King! He is crowned with many crowns, as "the kingdoms of this world is become the kingdoms of our Lord and of His Christ" (Rev. 11:15). We are living in the "King-Dominion."

During the reign of King Solomon, the Queen of Sheba visited him on a diplomatic trip. Having heard of his great kingdom, she found herself even more astonished when she saw it with her own eyes. (It takes a ruler to fully appreciate a kingdom.) One of the things she remarked about was "the food on his table, the seating of his officials, the attending servants in their robes, the cupbearers in their robes," et al. (2 Chr. 9:4).

The Queen was impacted by the wisdom of Solomon at first, but she was blown away by the majesty of his servants. Beloved, we are servants to one greater than Solomon. We are servants in the Great King's dominion and this should show in our lives—in how we treat others and how we handle "Kingdom-business." Oh, what a joy it will be when we fully come to know who we are! Be encouraged.

Be Prepared for Success

Keep falsehood and lies far from me; give me neither poverty nor riches, but give me only my daily bread. —Proverbs 30:8-9

God wants to bless you in an awesome way. This is part of His plan for the Body of Christ. He is placing wealth and influence into the hands of His saints in order to advance His kingdom.

We must be ready for our blessing. We must be prepared to manage God's blessings and be good stewards. We also must be ready to handle it emotionally. When God puts abundant resources at our fingertips, our disposition will change. If we think it will not, we will not be prepared.

We must learn the "good king's prayer" from the passage above. We must seek God continually that we not be deceived as His blessing flow to us. It is hard to pray for our daily bread when we already have a bakery. Yet, God is not blessing us to make what we are doing easier. He is simply preparing us to break into larger possibilities. Be ready for your blessing and be encouraged.

Failing Faith?

Be merciful to me, O Lord, for I am in distress; my eyes grow weak with sorrow, my soul and my body with grief. —Psalm 31:9

This verse in Psalm 31 begins a long litany of distressing confessions. David expresses his anguish and angst freely and openly to the Lord. Would you say from this that his faith in God has failed?

Extenuated sorrow and depression do represent a challenge to our faith system. We feel defeated and disoriented and dejected—David says, "I am forgotten by them as though I were dead; I have become like broken pottery" (Ps 31:12). But, this is not a denial of faith. We need to express our feelings to the Lord in order to get up from under them.

Now, faith is not denying the feeling that we have. It is overcoming them. We must hold to God's unchanging promises and confess them openly in bitter times. We must engage our feelings with the truth and boldly confess it. Then, with patience we can watch as God's faithfulness demolishes our deepest woes.

Be aware, there are times when your feelings become so oppressive that not one bit of God's past faithfulness will impress you. Yet, in your spirit you will know that He is faithful and you must base your life on the truth, not your feelings. You should be honest with your feelings, but then also know that they are but feelings. God's Word is the truth. Stand on it and be encouraged.

Awe of His Love

If you, O Lord, kept a record of sins, O Lord, who could stand? But with you there is forgiveness; therefore you are feared.
—Psalm 130:3-4

The love of Christ is awesome. Let us grow in our awareness of it. Just like launching out into deep waters—the further we go, the further we will see we have to go in it. It is simply beyond understanding.

I have sometimes a propensity to take Christ's love for granted. Yet, what always focuses me is when I see more of who Christ is. When I realize he came out of everlasting and went back into everlasting; when I consider the he sits at the right hand of majesty on high; when I see that God will judge the world through him and that he sees all my sins, I am infinitely impressed with my Jesus.

When one is impressed with Christ's largeness, it makes one consider one's smallness. Yet, Christ, with all that he is, considered our lives worth more than his own. How can we not stand in awe of his love? Be encouraged.

World Changers

...and if you spend yourselves in behalf of the hungry and satisfy the needs of the oppressed, then your light will rise in the darkness, and your night will become like the noonday. —Isaiah 58:10

God has a heart for the whole earth. I have touched this part of his heart and found there an ocean of grace and mercy. I bathed in it and it continues to refresh me in my daily walk in Christ.

We are compelled to attach ourselves to the big picture. We can navigate successfully through the forest of life only as we keep in our minds a sense of the landscape and for direction. Too many Christian hearts putter to the day to day malaise of "ordinary living," not realizing that every little thing they do can potentially have eternal significance.

You are a world changer. Your role may be simply to be a good husband, but you represent to the world Christ's love as you love your wife. You may be a homemaker, but you son may be the next great president. Take the little things you do seriously and never lose sight of the bigger picture. Be the world-changer you were meant to be and be encouraged.

Get Organized

There is a time for everything, and a season for every activity under heaven . . .
—Ecclesiastes 3:1

Dietrich Bonhoffer was a devout Christian who stood up against Adolf Hitler and his Nazi Party's atrocities in Germany. In that very pressing time, he realized the need for Christians to be effective in their witness in the world. As a part of his efforts, he wrote a book called, *Life Together*, and in it he dealt with the subject of personal organization.

The book is richly filled with principles and practical nuggets for personal development, but I want to extend one thought here: God is Lord over our personal time and we are accountable to Him as to how we use it. There are principles in the Scripture that instruct us in how we should use our mornings, afternoons and evenings; how we should set priorities; how and when we should work and rest; etc., etc.. We should recognize that the reigns controlling how we spent our time should be firmly in God's hands.

In our world today, we must have a very effective witness. To do this, we must be diligent in our time. May God help us all to submit thoroughly in this area. As always, be encouraged.

Souls

For God so loved the world that He gave His one and only Son that whoever would believe on Him would not perish, but have eternal life. —John 3:16

How are the souls of those around you doing where you are right now? There are really only two states of the soul—living or perishing. As we were saved, we were gifted with a spiritual barometer. It is just a matter of whether or not we use it.

I am more and more impressed in my spirit with a passion for souls. Our society is becoming darker by the minute. It is common for us to throw our concern at mass problems like poverty, school violence, AIDS, and the like. But, what about your neighbor who, on the surface, seems to be all right, but is perishing on the inside. What about your co-worker who's inward pain is so intense, they are willing to confide in you or just about anybody about very personal issues.

"The harvest is plentiful." This is not a phrase implying that there are many people out there who could fill up our churches or many hearts we could reach to mark a click on our Bibles. It means that there are many hearts ready for the message of God's love—many hearts that are perishing and without hope. One thing about a harvest—if you do not go out and get the crop, it will die. A great harvest of souls is upon us—let us be encouraged to reach them.

The Cry of Souls

The groans of the dying rise from the city, and the souls of the wounded cry out for help . . . —Job 24:12

We must hear the cry of souls. It amazes me that there are people who actually live life without hope, moving from day to day inwardly crushed by sin. Some put on fronts and others live openly dismayed and defeated. Yet, whether one admits it or not, the soul cries out for someone to help.

Beloved, we have a hope and a great salvation! The Lord promises a special peace—one unlike the world's circumstantial, ordinary peace—that can soak down into the depths of the souls and soothe its deepest achings. (John 14:27) For everyone that would come to him and live in the truth, his will is good, acceptable, and fulfilling. (Rom. 12:1-2) We have a holy balm for the wounded in the city. If only we would use it!

I am charged completely, dear friends, to hear the cry of souls. God has spoken and I am fearful to disappoint Him. And the passion that fills my soul at this moment is just what was needed to quench my heart's insatiable thirst for purpose. I have asked Christ to replace my chilly heart with a fleshy one that beats like His and He has done it! May He do this for you today as well.

Be encouraged.

Listen to the Spirit

But when he, the Spirit of truth, comes, he will guide you into all truth. He will not speak on his own; he will speak only what he hears, and he will tell you what is yet to come. —John 16:13

Listen to the Spirit. God's Holy Spirit has filled us as believers so that we may experience abundant life. He grants power for living and this power is significant for our Christian walk and witness. (Acts 1:8) God has given us the Spirit to lead us into all truth and thereby free us. Thus, we must be cautious to listen only to His voice.

There are other voices that purport to lead us in truth. The Bible says one of Satan's tricks is to accuse us—that is, to bring up evidence in our lives that we are not who God says we are. This evidence is often convincing and always convicting. Yet, no matter how true it may seem, it is not of God and we must not listen.

There are also the voices of the flesh. Pride, envy, bitterness and the like twist our perspective. This spawn of the flesh works actually to make the truth irrelevant. We can be brought to deny even the Word of God in order to fulfill the selfishness of the flesh. When our thoughts are at odds with God's words, we must humble ourselves quickly and submit to whatever God says.

The Holy Spirit has given us to lead us into truth. Learn to listen to Him. If your feelings are at odds with His voice, trust His gentleness. Confess it with your mouth out loud and resist the flesh and the devil. The Bible says clearly, "Since we live by the Spirit, let us keep in step with the Spirit" (Gal. 5:25). Follow this word and be encouraged.

The Spirit of Defeat

The man of God was angry with him and said, "You should have struck the ground five or six times; then you would have defeated Aram and completely destroyed it. But now you will defeat it only three times." —2 Kings 13:19

There is nothing more insidious than the spirit of defeat. This state of mind causes you to stop before reaching the finish line. Failure speaks to what you have done, but being defeated speaks to who you are. No Christian should for a moment tolerate this in their life!

Once there was a runner in a marathon. As everyone watched, he crossed the finish line well after most others in the race. By the time he finished, even the cadence of cheers for the winners had died out. He missed the fanfare and glory. He had worked hard and lost the race by an embarrassing margin.

After the race, a sportscaster wanted to interview a loser and see what their perspective of the race was. He asked the man what happened. Did he trip? The reply was, "No." Had he prepared enough? "Yes." Did he have some illness he was heroically facing? "No." Did he really want to win? "Yes." The reporter was thoroughly unimpressed with this runner until, as he began walking away, the man remarked, "I just can't wait to give it a shot next time."

Never let failures, fears or wounds from the past poison your spirit. Keep going. Get up and press on. God will give you a great victory if only you will believe.

Resources

*So Abraham called that place The Lord
Will Provide. And to this day it is said,
"On the mountain of the Lord it will be
provided." —Genesis 22:14*

God's resources are our resources. Because of His
tremendous love for us he has set this promise in
Christ, "I tell you the truth, my Father will give you
whatever you ask in my name." God has set provision for us for every challenge and is prepared for
our request even before we ask.

The Father's resources are awesome. The Bible
says, "The earth is the LORD's, and everything in it,
the world, and all who live in it" (Ps. 24:1). Again
God says, "If I were hungry I would not tell you, for
the world is mine, and all that is in it" (Ps. 50:12)
Our Lord closes his great model prayer with "For
yours is the kingdom and the power and the glory
forever" (Matt. 6:13, KJV). Again the Scriptures say,
"The kingdom of the world has become the kingdom
of our Lord and of his Christ, and he will reign forever and ever" (Rev 11:15). God has no lack.

We, however, lack when we do not trust and serve
the Lord. The bad part about it is that when we suffer want, it makes us less and less willing to trust—
and it is exactly trusting the Lord that will relieve our
want.

My dear friends, save yourselves from this cycle

of defeat. Trust the Lord and do not doubt. He has prepared so much for you and you will have it if you only believe.

Be encouraged.

Fallen

Then the eyes of both of them were opened, and they realized they were naked; so they sewed fig leaves together and made coverings for themselves. —Genesis 3:7

This is a generation spoiled by temptation. It is flaunted and magnified. It is almost all-pervasive. No more does Satan uses subtleness and cunning. All is blatant and out in the open, threatening to make us more callous to wickedness.

Have you been ridiculed for your stance of faith? Are you threatened with ostracization because you hold fast to your standards? Beloved, be very careful not to nuzzle with this fallen world. You are the light and, though at first you may be passed off or condemned, you have within you the answer for which the world has been looking.

You are the head, not the tail. Why follow? It is your time to lead. Let us not fear ridicule or even persecution for the Lord's sake. With all gentleness and love, let us hold fast to the truth never, never give in. This world is fallen, we should not be. Be encouraged.

Behold His Glory

. . . We have seen his glory, the glory of the One and Only, who came from the Father, full of grace and truth. —John 1:14

There is a glory in Christ Jesus that must be seen. This glory was intentionally hidden from view as the Word was made flesh. Yet, unto those that were "taught of God" (John 6:45) and pursued Him, God revealed it. Our relationship with Christ is dependant on our seeing this glory.

Who is Christ to you? Is he your "Lord" or your "LORD?" Do you reverence him with awe, our is he more like a heavenly friend? I am charged, beloved, to see him for who he really is.

Consider this proverb: the Lamb is a Lion. When you see the Lion in the Lamb, you will be well on your way to newness and freshness in God. Be aware, beloved, and be encouraged.

A Jesus Feeling

That which was from the beginning, which we have heard, which we have seen with our eyes, which we have looked at and our hands have touched– this we proclaim concerning the Word of life. —1 Jn 1:1

Closeness to the Lord brings about a distinct "Jesus feeling." We cannot touch him with any of our natural senses. Yet, when we are involved in sharing our faith and in acts of love, we experience him. This is to say that when we live his life, we experience his closeness.

This kind of closeness to the Master is priceless. Many have given their hopes, dreams, personal aspirations and even their very lives pursuing it. I am not referring to an obsession with spiritual experiences when I speak of this. We can have wonderful religious experiences that have nothing to do with a true closeness to God. Beware of these! Closeness to Jesus is accomplished through a duration and enduring faith and a faithfulness to fulfill his work in the earth.

Beloved, there is something more than what many of us are partaking. There is an indomitable faith. There is true victory over life's circumstances. There is power from heaven that can change the earth. There is a true "Jesus feeling" that gives so much purpose that we will willingly surrender our lives. Be encouraged to find it and walk in it.

The Power of Encouragement

Therefore encourage each other with these words. —1 Thessalonians 4:18

Encouragement is a great power for the sake of the gospel. When we share our faith in Christ, we do it for compassion's sake. God has raised Christ and us in him to demonstrate His dynamic love for the world. Therefore, the tools and methods by which we share the good news must reflect this love.

Encouragement is a tremendous way of loving. It seeks to uplift the heart and empower people to be their best. Everyone loves an encourager. He or she brightens up a room and sweetens a conversation. Encouragement is medicine to the soul.

In urge you today to take up the task of encouragement. Find something positive in someone and uplift them by drawing attention to it. Think on the goodness of life in Christ and declare its beauty. Find a poor soul and let them know they are not alone. Encourage someone today, and be encouraged.

In These Days

You must be on your guard. You will be handed over to the local councils and flogged in the synagogues. On account of me you will stand before governors and kings as witnesses to them. —Mark 13:9

Many of us feel excessive pressure as we live out our faith in Christ. What does it mean when we do our best to serve Him, only to be faced with loss and troubles? What can be said when we set our hearts to serve Him only to find ourselves faltering and consequently discouraged? My friends, there is hope in God.

Let us uphold the right perspective. Jesus said both: "In this world you will have trial and tribulation, but be of good cheer—I have overcome the world" (John 16:33), and "I have come that you might have [life more abundantly]" (John 10:10b). Both are true. Beloved, the abundant life consists not in escaping challenge and trouble; it lies firmly in facing it and, by God's unmerited favor, overcoming it. Do not turn away from hardship; it pleases the Lord for you and I to make it through it.

In a soon coming day, we will stand the pressure of witnessing before "governors and kings" (whoever these may represent) and be used mightily of the Spirit. Souls will be reached and saved because of what we endure now. God is preparing us in the crucible of life so that our truest worth may be made manifest. We may find the lies of the world easier to take for the moment; but they are arsenic and we have seen enough of their results.

Be encouraged!

Do What It Takes

Do your best to present yourself to God as one approved, a workman who does not need to be ashamed and who correctly handles the word of truth. —2 Timothy 2:15

We must do what it takes to walk victoriously in Christ. It takes a good deal of preparation and we must immerse ourselves in the Scriptures. Maturity in Christ does not come in a day, but it will come with enough exposure in God's Word.

We must learn to think as Christians. God wants to transform not only what we think about, but how we think. He does not want our hearts without our minds or our minds without our hearts. God wants it all.

Think about this. Most of the time when we find ourselves inwardly defeated or frustrated, it is because we have failed to see things in terms of God's Word. God's Word gives perspective and motivation and power. Have you done what it takes?

Be encouraged.

Friends for Life

My intercessor is my friend as my eyes pour out tears to God; on behalf of a man he pleads with God as a man pleads for his friend. —Job 16:20-21

Many people enter our lives, but some are put there by God. We need to recognize the friends that God has given us. These relationships are given to us to enhance our lives.

You may not talk all the time with your God-given friend. You may have different interests and it might be that you spend very little time together. But you know that friend is praying for you and you are encouraged in your heart at every thought of him or her.

Thank God for your truest friends today and be encouraged.

Pride

*The Lord detests all the proud of heart. Be
sure of this: They will not go unpunished.
—Proverbs 16:5*

It is common for us to recognize that God hates a proud look. (Prov. 6:17) Yet, we must realize that He hates pride down to its roots. The roots of pride lie buried deep in our hearts. We may often cut the stem of pride, but like a springtime weed it will always grow back again. We must allow the Lord to destroy it deep down.

The process to destroy our pride is accomplished by God and God alone. We cannot do this thing. The extent of our efforts must be in prayer alone. The rest of the work belongs to the Master. God destroys pride in us in many different ways. Through sporadic failures and carefully orchestrated moments of desperation, God extracts the line of pride from us.

We must understand that pride is insidious and be aware that it can come up when we least expect it. Never think you've got it licked, for it is easy to get it going and hard to stop it. Just trust day by day in God's process and learn not to complain. He will be persistent to deliver you.

Be encouraged.

We Fall Down

For though a righteous man falls seven times, he rises again, but the wicked are brought down by calamity. —Proverbs 24:16

Though we may fall many times, we can always get up. Our righteousness before God is won by faith. It is not a self-righteousness based on perfection of performance. It is a righteousness that God declares because we have trusted in Him.

Avoid the trap of performance. What do you think? If you cajole yourself enough and chastise yourself, do you think this will produce better performance? It will not. Yet, if you trust in the living God, He will bring out of you your best. God has filled you with a greatness that comes from His grace. When you keep trusting Him, though you fall, He will patiently teach you and build you up.

I have often inwardly wished that things in my life could have been done more perfectly. Yet, God's grace has always met me in those moments and called me to trust Him still. And now, in retrospect, most of my greatest lessons were afforded me after I had fallen.

Many, many years ago, a great Christian leader named Martin Luther once said, "Sin boldly." He obviously was not advocating unrighteousness. Rather, he was saying that when we fall, we have a powerful advocate with the Father and he has won our right to get up again. Be encouraged.

A Passion for Souls

God, whom I serve with my whole heart in preaching the gospel of his Son, is my witness how constantly I remember you . . .
—*Romans 1:9*

I began writing these encouragements several year ago to help some of my dear friends (as well as myself) to hold fast to a passion for Jesus Christ and a passion for souls. This ministry has grown since I started and I am more honored to be used in this way than I can really say. I genuinely hope that your quest for the things of God has been strengthen.

The passion of souls begins like this ministry began. It begins with remembering others. When we take the time to remember the few people God has placed in our path, our lists will grow. Paul had a "whole heart" for the gospel truth, but it would have been hard to maintain his passion if he neglected to think of those that God put in his life.

God has filled your life with people to remember for the sake of the gospel. Who are they? Whoever they may be, take the time to pray for them. Ask God for an open door. Be patient and leave things up into God's hand. Do not be so goal-achievement oriented. Fulfill your passion one bit at a time. The Bible says, "Constantly remember . . . ." Remember and be encouraged.

Spiritual Motivation

Grace and peace be yours in abundance through the knowledge of God and of Jesus our Lord. His divine power has given us everything we need for life and godliness through our knowledge of him who called us by his own glory and goodness. Through these he has given us his very great and precious promises, so that through them you may participate in the divine nature and escape the corruption in the world caused by evil desires. —2 Peter 1:2-4

Have you ever wondered what motivated Paul or what was the driving force for Peter? How could Stephen in the book of Acts have so much peace when they were stoning him to death? Why would John endure being whipped, ostracized, and even boiled in a pot of oil for the gospel? I believe some of this motivation is revealed in Peter's words here.

The early fathers and mothers of the Church were driven and endured hardship because they experienced something—Paul called it, "the excellency of the knowledge of Him." (Phil. 3:8) The passage above teaches us that the more we get to truly know Him, the more the divine power of God is poured out in our lives.

We experience God in Christ through things like

study, obedience, faith, worship, prayer, and thanks-giving. The more we "participate in the divine nature," we can know the joy of overcoming discouragement, hardships, trails, and doubts. Be encouraged.

Direction

...in the first year of his reign, I, Daniel, understood from the Scriptures, according to the word of the Lord given to Jeremiah the prophet, that the desolation of Jerusalem would last seventy years. So I turned to the Lord God and pleaded with him in prayer and petition, in fasting, and in sackcloth and ashes. —Dan 9:2-3

God directs his people. We have an assurance that if we acknowledge him in all our ways, He will direct our path. This is the assurance that Daniel was operating in. In this story, Daniel sought the Lord about an issue and eventually the answer came. We can learn from Daniel's methods how we too can receive direction from God.

1) Daniel searched the Scriptures. Faith is not based on conjecture. It is based on the solidity of God's Word. When you want to know a thing, seek what the Scriptures say about it first.

2) Daniel prayed the Scripture. We must discover God's plan and promises in the Scriptures and begin to pray them for our lives. This sets us in the right direction and begins to make clear how we are to proceed.

3) Daniel pleaded with God in three ways. With "prayer and petition," Daniel opened the matter up to God. We should make specific requests. As we do,

God will help clarify what the real issues are. With fasting, Daniel denied himself. When we seek direction concerning a thing, we should take ourselves out of it as best we can. With "sackcloth and ashes" Daniel abased himself. We need to acknowledge our sinfulness and unworthiness to receive God's blessing, even as we share our need for it.

Daniel approached God with directness, honesty and in the right spirit. He did not ask God and then try to answer for God. He did not doubt that God would answer (he waited 21 days with fasting and in dirty clothes!). And Daniel got his answer. May you know the joy of answered prayer as He did.

No Condemnation

Therefore, there is now no condemnation for those who are in Christ Jesus.
—Romans 8:1

It could be easy to think that there is no condemnation for us, just so long as we walk in a particular way—or, just so long as we act right. This is not the sense of this verse. Paul is saying, everyone who is in Christ Jesus has received the Holy Spirit in their lives (vv. 2, 15), and, in effect, the Spirit works in us to will and do God's good pleasure. (v.11 cf. Phil. 2:13).

This is the cornerstone of your victory over sin. Your victory begins with a faith and assurance in the God that has saved you, is leading you in the right way, and, in the process, does not condemn you.

You do not overcome sin by trusting in your own ability to do what God's says is right. This is trusting in your flesh. The Bible says, instead, to trust in the work of the Holy Spirit without deceit. In other words, do not say, "the Spirit is working on me" and use that as an excuse to sin or to just have your own way (this would make you a liar and the Spirit of truth would not be in you).

Trust in the work of God's Spirit in your life. This is how you receive the ability and desire to put to stop your own selfish, sinful works and to live a life with passion unto God.

May the Spirit of the living God set you on fire today.

November 30

The Gospel of Victory

But thanks be to God! He gives us the victory through our Lord Jesus Christ. —1 Corinthians 15:57

The intended result of the gospel is victory. It is not a victory that we win; it is a victory that has been won for us. God gives us victory through His Son Jesus Christ. This is a truth the body of Christ must put to use!

As a Christian, you have victory in your life. Though you may fall, you are never down for the count. Though you may fail, you can never be written off. Though you may suffer, you are never alone. Your life in Christ is not tied up in what you accomplish for him (or for yourself). It is firmly set by what he has accomplished for you and the grace from God that his finished work affords.

I am a living testimony of God's redeeming grace. No matter how I mess up, he keeps on doing great things for me. This does not give me encouragement to sin. The Bible says we are dead to sin. (Rom. 6:1-6) Rather it gives me confidence to stretch out in Him and be who He has called me to be. May you share this confidence as well.

Be encouraged.

Possessing Mind of Christ

Let this mind be in you, which was also in Christ Jesus. —Philippians 2:5 (KJV)

As I began to concentrate on possessing the mind of Christ, I learned a few principles that I pray may be a blessing to you. These come from an examination of Philippians 2:5-13.

1. Christ understood who he was, but did not take himself too seriously. I learned that as Jesus, the second person in the Godhead, disregarded his position and great stature to become a humble, obedient servant, I too should not think too highly of myself. I have learned to ask myself when getting praise or pummeled with criticism, "Who am I to get so much attention?"

2. God raises up those who willingly die to themselves. We die to ourselves by giving way to a greater purpose, even if it causes us to suffer or go without. Jesus did more than just leave his glory and come to the earth. He went through more than thirty years saying to the Father, "Not my will, but Thine be done."

3. Obedience + the Fear of the Lord = Powerful Godliness. Our sense of obedience to God and God's Word must be coupled with a healthy sense of who God is. The fear of the Lord is not mistrusting His anger like a child with a drunken parent. It is having a healthy regard for His awesome presence and power.

I hope and pray these thoughts will spur you on to a greater walk with God. Trust me, the experience is worth it.

Sabbath Rest

*Also I gave them my Sabbaths as a sign
between us, so they would know that I the
Lord made them holy. —Ezekiel 20:12*

Rest is a most important aspect of Christian living.
The Scripture above teaches us that God made rest a
requirement for His covenant people. In fact, their
restfulness and peacefulness were to be a sign to
other nations and peoples that there was something
special about them—indeed, it was a sign of their
special relationship with God.

We often downplay the importance of rest. Our
busy schedules quickly push out our resting time.
One day I watched a little baby struggling to stay
awake. What is it about our world today that even in
our earliest years, we learn to disregard and fight
rest? Whatever the answer to this question is, God
wants us to give ourselves to rest.

Rest comes ultimately from trusting God. Often
we work so hard and reject resting because we are
often anxious and worried. Rest comes when we can
LET THINGS GO. This is hard in our fast-paced
lives.

Be relieved in knowing that our Father is working
as we work. (John 5:17) Stop trying to make things
happen and trust that when you have done all you
can do, God goes before and follows-up after you.

Let your anxiety go. With all you have to do, you

do not need worry on top of it. Learn to trust in the Master and in "all things by prayers and supplications with thanksgivings, let your request be made known to God." (Phil. 4:6)

May this bless your life.

Silence

". . . a time to tear and a time to mend, a time to be silent and a time to speak . . ."
—Ecclesiastes 3:7

It has been said that silence is golden. Silence is an asset to rest. We all want a quiet moment sometimes. Silence quiets inside noise as well as outside. We must value this silence if we will walk closer to the Lord.

The great prophet Elijah had to learn the value of silence. There was a time when the prophet was riddled with anxiety and deep questions. God led him to a cave in the jagged face of Mt. Sinai and gave him three signs. The first sjgn was a tempest. The second, an earthquake. The third, a great fire. Elijah expected God to come in these great and powerful manifestations like He has done before, but God did not. For him a new lesson was to be learned.

After the wind, quake and inferno there was silence. This silence was powerful after so much commotion. It was in this great silence that God spoke, gave him clear direction, and put his world back together.

We must learn this lesson. Seek the powerful silence of the soul. Find a place, if but for a few moments, to gather yourself and sit with God in comfort. God's grace will minister to you in this place. God will speak to you, like He did with Elijah, in powerful ways you would never expect.

May the peace of God fill you with a great passion for life.

Wholeness

*I have been crucified with Christ and I no
longer live, but Christ lives in me. The life
I live in the body, I live by faith in the Son
of God, who loved me and gave himself for
me. —Galatians 2:20*

Watchman Nee, a hero of faith, was laid up in a
brutal Chinese Prison for nearly forty years. The the
countries Communist Party imprisoned him on
trumped up charges because he would not deny
Christ. He endured many unspeakable tortures during these prison years, yet his enduring peace and
joy in the Lord is legendary.

Nee's strength of character did not come in a day.
A definitive moment for him was toward the beginning of his ministry, as he faced a debilitative heart
condition. He cried out for healing and it did not
come to him. He struggled with bouts of depression
over his failed prayers and soon thought to give up
his ministry and maybe even his faith.

One day as he walked a paved walkway on the side
of a craggy mountain that towered over a beautiful
lake, he considered the beauty born out of Christ's
brokenness. Then, he made a decision. He would stop
wavering with every wind and circumstance. If he
would die, he would die in Christ; if he would live, he
would live in Christ. Nee slammed his walking stick
into a crack in the walkway and marched off.

Moments later and only steps away, he began again with his doubts and depression. But, with a sense of violence and vengeance he turned around and pointed to his abandoned crutch and declared, "No, I will leave you there!" He developed wholeness at the point he put down his cane and picked up his cross. We too must lay down our crutch of depression and grab tightly to the crosses we must bear.

Be encouraged.

Praise the Lord

*Clap your hand all ye people, shout unto
God with the voice of triumph. —Psalm
47:1 (KJV)*

There were times when David or the other
psalmists did not feel like praising God. David wrote
many lamenting psalms explaining to God his troubles and his inability to doing anything about them.
Take a look at the Book of Psalms and see how many
you can find. He starts off with something like: "O
God have mercy on your servant," or "Hear, O God,
your servant's plea." Yet, with one or two excep-
tions, David always ends the psalm in praise. This is
amazing.

The fact is, as David wrote and sung, his attention
would move from himself to the awesomeness of
God. Take a look at the verse following today's
Scripture: "How awesome is the LORD Most High,
the great King over all the earth!" As David voiced
the details of his problems and, then, considered the
greatness of God, he moved from victim status to
victory.

Facing our problems and wretchedness sometimes
helps us face the Lord. For as we consider our limitations, our inabilities, and our "finite-ness," we can
realize more that the only way we have gotten this
far is through His power, His grace and His wisdom.

May He strengthen you in your spirit today!

Serious Power

*Then the Spirit of the Lord came upon him
in power. —Judges 14:19*

The price of spiritual power is in taking time with God. In this we show that we take Him seriously. Yet, this is the issue for most of us. We never seem to have enough time. We must learn as did the men and women of God in the Bible how to give our time to the Father.

Jesus as a rule prayed often late into the night and early in the morning. (Mark 1:35; Luke 6:12) Truly no one of us may claim to be busier than he, but his culture provided for rest periods throughout the day. He also maintained good physical stamina through all the walking he did. Such is important for operating on shorter hours of sleep. The prophetess Anna "never left the temple but worshiped night and day, fasting and praying" (Luke 2:37). Some are truly called to the vocation of prayer. We rarely see this in our culture, yet we rarely see dynamic displays of God's power as well. Daniel worked a high-stress job, but found time with God morning, noon and night. (Dan. 6:10) He also fasted from meats and sweets. This provided nourishment to keep up his daily schedule and yet maintained the self-effacement involved in fasting and mourning. (Dan. 10:3)

Our Lord and these others were not too busy to pray. They were too busy not to pray. We are too used to doing things in our own strength. How much time do you need if you have the power from on high aiding you? Be encouraged.

Faith Does

He chose to be mistreated along with the people of God rather than to enjoy the pleasures of sin for a short time.
—Hebrews 11:25

Faith is what faith does. The Bible shows us over and again that separation between faith and works is rhetorical only. In other words, we may know that faith alone connects us to our salvation, yet that faith will be shown in what we do with our lives. One most important area in which our faith is worked out is in our relationships.

We can see what we believe through our relationships. The Bible says, "The only thing that counts is faith expressing itself through love" (Gal. 5:6). When our faith is in Christ, we yearn and seek to love others. When we are unsuccessful in this, our hearts are convicted and, by God's Spirit, we are moved to make amends. You cannot encounter the omnipotent love of God and not desire to truly love in every relationship you have.

Beware my friends of allowing your love to grow cold. If you do this, you deceive yourself and you do not walk by faith. This is a generation where "the love of most will grow cold" (Matt. 24:12). It is easy to become unloving and complacent because "everybody's doing it." Let your life instead be a light. Be counter-cultural. Love all the more. As you do, people will see your faith and give glory to the God that made it possible.

Be encouraged.

Witnessing Authority

When the crowd saw this, they were filled with awe; and they praised God, who had given such authority to men. —Matthew 9:8

God has given us great power in witnessing to others. This power is represented through answered prayer, strong character, and through the gifts of the Spirit. We cannot effectively witness without the power from God. Yet, even with this great power, if we do not walk with authority, power will have little effect.

A Christian without authority is like a general untrained in battle or a police officer afraid to use his firearm. What would it matter if you had all the power in the world and you failed to use it? Authority is knowing when, where and how to use your power.

When we witness, we must be bold and truthful. We do not have to argue with people. If we speak the words of Christ, they will speak for themselves. God himself will back up His words. We must witness with words of authority knowing that God grants power to back them up. Walk in your authority and be encouraged.

Expect More

*When Jesus heard this, he was astonished
and said to those following him, "I tell you
the truth, I have not found anyone in Israel
with such great faith. —Matthew 8:10*

What do you expect from God? It seems more and
more so many expect less and less from Him. With a
God so awesome, why should we lack anything we
need? And why should Jesus ever be astonished
among his people to find great faith?

A young man once told the story of his encounter
with God. It started with his determination to know
God in the power of His glory. It took him years of
prayer and fasting and seeking God, but gradually
and powerfully his wish was granted. He expected
something from God and actively waited on him
until it came to pass. What great faith!

Should we learn to expect more from God, we
would receive more through persistence. Could it be
the power you need to do what you yearn to do waits
upon your faith to be applied with commitment?
Could it really be that God has much more to pour
out in your life than what you currently see? Expect
more, beloved, and be encouraged.

The Saving Power of Faith

I say to you that many will come from the east and the west, and will take their places at the feast with Abraham, Isaac and Jacob in the kingdom of heaven. But the subjects of the kingdom will be thrown outside, into the darkness, where there will be weeping and gnashing of teeth.
—Matthew 8:11-12

It is a terrifying notion to me to read "the subjects of the kingdom will be thrown outside." Yet, the truth is, all that are in the church will not see the kingdom. Who shall see the kingdom and how shall we know them? Truly the just will live by their faith. (Hab. 2:4)

We have made faith too much an issue of theory. It is not academic and sterile. It is lively and powerful. We come to know what faith is not simply by definition, but also by example. We are told of the faith of Abel who gave his best and the faith of Enoch who did all to please God. Before us is Noah who feared and obeyed God's Word and Abraham who sacrificed all to follow Him. Abraham's wife waited upon God's miracle and, by faith, his son Isaac spoke into his generations. We can go on and on to see what real faith is and to see that it has always saved.

Real faith honors God as God. True faith submits

to and exercises divine authority. Faith is not just about believing or doing what is right. It is about living out what is right through the power and grace of God. Do not rest in anything else beloved, and be encouraged.

Grace and Power

I became a servant of this gospel by the gift of God's grace given me through the working of his power. —Ephesians 3:7

Salvation works many things in our lives. We may know through it that all our sins are forgiven and will be forgiven in Christ. We may rejoice in the Psalm, "Blessed is he whose transgressions are forgiven, whose sins are covered" (Ps. 32:1). We may also know that, as this is so, "God's power works in us to will and to do his good pleasure" (Phil. 2:13) As His grace wipes clean our slate, His power causes us to fulfill what is right in our lives.

Our forgiveness is the undeniable work of the Cross, but it is not the only work. Praise God for this, for as we lose the fear of God's wrath and punishment, we regain the ability to walk in power and purpose. Think of this, God not only delivers us from sin, but delivers us to abundant life.

The Bible says, "For the message of the cross is foolishness to those who are perishing, but to us who are being saved it is the power of God" (1 Cor. 1:18). Think on these things and be encouraged.

Little Things

I thank God, whom I serve, as my forefathers did, with a clear conscience, as night and day I constantly remember you in my prayers. —2 Timothy 1:3

We should learn to appreciate those who God has placed in our lives. Many times we fail to tell people how much they mean to us. I for one, have been terrible at this. But, praise God for the leading of his Spirit.

Be sensitive to the Spirit when He leads you in the little things. Maybe He is telling you to get a card for someone. Maybe a coworker can use some unsolicited encouragement. Maybe your son or daughter would benefit from your view of all that they can be. The little things mean so very much.

I encourage you to build an empire on the little things. Buy stacks of cards at a time. Write down and remember birthdays. Greet people with a "God bless you." Visit a nursing home. Join an intercessory prayer group. The most beautiful buildings are made with small bricks. Show appreciation for people and let the love of God flow through you.

Be encouraged.

The Value of Salvation

For I am not seeking my own good but the good of many, so that they may be saved.
—1 Corinthians 10:33

We must increase our estimation of the value of salvation. Where is the passion for souls? What of spiritual fervor? We must not settle for building kingdoms on the earth. We must proclaim Christ's kingdom here on earth, for it is coming and is at hand as we speak of it.

The Bible says that God has put eternity in the hearts of all living souls. Yet, for more than many of us eternity seems far, far away. Some of us have lost hope that there is meaning beyond this life. This is tragic. God loves us and His love is not just a fling. He loves us for forever.

As amazing it may seem, everyone does not know this forever-kind-of-love. Without His love in their hearts, people will be lost and eternity will prove to be a living hell. Think about what you have, beloved, and if this thought blesses you, share it with someone else. Be encouraged.

Courage Under Fire

Be on your guard; stand firm in the faith; be men of courage; be strong.
—*1 Corinthians 16:13*

The enemy will do everything in his power to terrorize us. Yet, as children of God we have a constitution resistant to this. It is time for us to understand our power over fear.

The Bible teaches that our faith gives us victory over fear. It causes us to "long for a better country—a heavenly one" (Heb. 11:16). It ties our hearts and our hopes to the unstoppable fulfillment of God's promise to one day set things in order from above. As we stand in this hope, we have a confidence that even death cannot take away. And once we are free from the fear of death, we can truly live.

Do not let fear overwhelm you. You are made for greater things than what this world has to offer and God has set you in this world to show that these greater things exist. Take courage now, beloved, for now is a time for you to shine.

In all things, be encouraged.

Walls and Gates

"The wall of Jerusalem is broken down, and its gates have been burned with fire."
—Nehemiah 1:3

In ancient times, walls and gates were used by cities for protection. The huge stone structures outlined the city borders, keeping what was bad out and what was good in. The gates provided access and were opened at will to friends. Our souls are like these ancient cities, with walls of protection and gates. Our walls are made of character and our relationships are our gates.

For some of us, our walls are broken down—meaning, our character has failed in some way. Our character fails when we sin. When this happens we find ourselves constantly in trouble and affliction. For some of us, our gates are burned. Because of this, we spill our hearts to the wrong people and have trouble setting boundaries in our lives. Either we are overbearing or we let others walk all over us.

God says, "righteousness guards the man of integrity, but wickedness overthrows the sinner" (Prov. 13:6). Let us all study the Word and learn the way of God. We can deliver ourselves from incessant troubles. We must always trust the Spirit in directing the company we keep. By these means, we will win great peace for our souls.

Be encouraged.

December 16

Don't Give In

The sluggard craves and gets nothing, but the desires of the diligent are fully satisfied. —Proverbs 13:4

Giving in to defeat is a sign of spiritual laziness. We need learn to keep our mind exercised and trained on God's Word. The fact of the matter is, if you try you cannot lose. Do not give in.

It takes work to maintain a stance of faith and it is worth it. Things will not always feel right and this can drain you of energy. You must in the face of this declare your victory. Then, from the power you harness from this, be diligent in your task.

Listen, beloved, we must start dealing with the big tasks in our lives. Do not be discouraged when the task seems too hard. God will help you. Just be diligent and focused. Prepare yourself. Plan your work and work your plan. Do this and true satisfaction will be yours.

Spiritual Organization

Evening, morning and noon I cry out in distress, and he hears my voice. —Psalm 55:17

It is important to have an organized prayer life. Pray in all situations and with all dispatch whenever a need arises. Yet, train yourself to set special times throughout the day to steal away for greater concentration and focus in prayer. With so many issues pressing upon us, we must find our stability and strength through spiritual organization.

In this fast-paced world, you must be equipped to deal with many different situations all at once. There are times when while we focus on one thing, two others sideswipe us. This is the enemy's ploy to get us out of our spiritual flow. We are drawn from trusting God's strength when we start reacting to things that unexpectedly come up in our life.

Set your mind, therefore, to spend some time centering yourself in God. Take time before breakfast and after lunch to go over your day with Him. Reflect with Him during the early evening and use this time to prepare for the next day. This requires discipline. We must make ourselves do this at all costs. The dividends of this practice will bring much success to our lives.

Be encouraged.
EARLIER

Power and Authority

They had Peter and John brought before them and began to question them: "By what power or what name did you do this?" —Acts 4:7

God has given us both power and authority to accomplish His work in the earth. To be clear, this power is miracle working and fully impacting and effectual. It should not be written off or made to mean something else. Coupled with this effectual power is the authority to use Jesus' Name.

Where is the power God has given us now? In truth, it is too rarely seen. It is displayed more in circles that are markedly less commercial than the average American church or ministry. It is a frightful thing to market the power of God! (Acts 6:17-23) I do not believe God gives much power to those who will not wait on Him and operate for Him and as He would please.

Amazingly, we also see too little of the great authority given to the saints. What many often see is a bold display of Christ-like authority inside the four walls of the church. This is a sham and a shame. (Indeed, I too have been subject to this sham at times.)

Truly, we must rise to the point spiritually that we will not settle for less than God's true gift of power and authority. The world will resist, but our reach must be lengthened the distance only these things can provide. Let us be encouraged to seek God more earnestly.

Leaning on Power

. . . but wait for the gift my Father promised, which you have heard me speak about. —Acts 1:4

Have you learned how to wait on God? His power is available to impact your life and living. If you want to really see it, you must learn how to wait.

Waiting is the chief thing in the process of leaning on God. It does not connote inactivity. Rather, waiting suggests something different. In a familiar sense of the word, to wait on someone is to serve them. Waiting on God carries this kind of meaning. While we wait, we must live out godly principles and serve God through others.

The disciples waited on God by gathering together for prayer and organizing themselves for what God was going to do. Then, the Holy Spirit came with great power on the day of Pentecost. Let us likewise wait for great power through prayer and preparation. I have learned, God is not expecting us to do the thing, He simply wants us to be ready when He does. Be encouraged.

Living By Power

Since we live by the Spirit, let us keep in step with the Spirit. —Galatians 5:25

The Spirit of God gives us power as Christians to be witnesses of Christ and His Kingdom. We are witnesses through living and giving. Christ is shown by the example of our lives and also through loving service. The Spirit enables our living and giving, renewing our hearts and adding grace to our service.

Our hearts are renewed when the Spirit equips by renewing our spirit. This is grace's first work. Afterward, God gives of mighty gifts, talents and abilities to fulfill His work and show his power in our lives.

Sometimes the Body of Christ is divided because we do not understand God's power and emphasize one aspect against the other. Both are necessary—the living and the giving—to be effective witnesses in the earth.

Be encouraged.

Walking By Power

> *Jesus replied, "You are in error because you do not know the Scriptures or the power of God." —Matthew 22:29*

We cannot by our own power live the Christian life. It is designed that way. Should we desire to truly walk as Christians, we must walk with faith in God's power.

God's Word is the foundation of our faith. God's power is the cornerstone of our Christian walk. We serve a living God who is more than able to impact our lives and our world. God's power is not simply displayed through random miracles and acts of nature. It can be depended upon. There are ways and times you can expect to see it.

We see God's power in our lives predictably when we walk according to God's Word. His Word always calls us to do things we would or could not do due to weakness in our character or personal abilities. It calls us to see impossible situations become possible through acts of faith. It causes us to love radically and vulnerably without fear. God's Word makes us stretch our imagination and sense of our possibilities.

When we stretch out with faith in God's direction, we run into God's power every time. Let the power of God impact your life like never before today. Be encouraged.

What Do You Know?

[He] asked them, "Did you receive the Holy Spirit when you believed?" They answered, "No, we have not even heard that there is a Holy Spirit." —Acts 19:2

Sometimes we get so set in our ways that we miss fresh understanding of the Word of God. Sometimes in an attempt not to be like this or that group of people, we lose our ability to receive the Word for what it is. Sometimes in our knowledge we condemn ourselves to ignorance. I say, let the Word speak for itself.

God has given us His Spirit to empower our living and giving. The Spirit affects our character and increases our capabilities. He is God's choicest gift to us while we are yet on earth, but so many of us miss benefitting from this gift.

I encourage you today to read God's Word with fresh vigor and an open mind. Do not rationalize God's wonders away. See how God enabled and empowered early believers and see if you are walking in this level of power and effectiveness. If you are not, you can be. Be encouraged.

Healing: The True Meaning of Christmas

"She will give birth to a son, and you are to give him the name Jesus, because he will save his people from their sins."
—Matthew 1:21

God sent His Son into the world to heal. Healing is not simply a physical thing. We all have needed it physical, emotionally, psychologically and spiritually. Many of us need it at this moment.

We are wounded, crushed, or dismayed because of sin in our lives. Bad choices, wrong motives, harbored resentments, untended hurts, phony facades, untoward behaviors, swelled ego, proud looks, shallow conscience, false remorse, and the like are all examples of the sin that wounds us. Unchecked, sin will mortally wound us.

It is hard to face up to facts when we are sick. It is all the more difficult for us to be real about the sin in our lives. But, we must confess our malady, if we are to be cured by God's divine grace. To be honest, though I know this and have preached it often, I sometimes need reminding. This is one reason why we celebrate Christmas.

Remember the reason for the season and be encouraged.

Merry Christmas

For to us a child is born, to us a son is given, and the government will be on his shoulders. And he will be called Wonderful Counselor, Mighty God, Everlasting Father, Prince of Peace. —Isaiah 9:6

This prophetic word extending from the 8th Century before Christ transcends time. It spoke specifically to the birth of our Lord Christ about 2000 years ago, but it also speaks to us today. Unto US a child IS born.

From the foundation of the world, God provided an answer to the problems He knew beforehand that we would face. God is never left wondering what to do. He has had the answer form the beginning.

The Child is born to be a savior and for us to put our lives into his hand. The government of our lives is to be on His shoulders. I challenge you to use this Christmas as a time of reflection. Leave some rest time amid the hustle and bustle of the season to consider some things. Is your life in his hands? Is it squarely on his shoulders?

Merry Christmas. Be encouraged.

Overcoming Debt

So if you have not been trustworthy in handling worldly wealth, who will trust you with true riches? —Luke 16:11

Many of us probably think we are in better shape financially than we really are. We reason to ourselves, "as long as I can make the payments. . . ." Yet, what we are doing is putting ourselves more and more into the slavery of debt. So, when God is ready to use us, we are inundated and loaded down by a heavy weight.

I have come to know three sins that undergird our ensuing bondage to debt: 1) poor planning for immediate and long-term needs, 2) ignorance and foolishness in ultimately thinking we would get something for nothing, 3) indulgence of our fleshly want and desires. You may be under one, two or all of these categories.*

I encourage you to come to terms with your debt, your self, and your sin. Confess your sins and repent. God will surely bring you out. I am going to say two things that are bold, but I base my very life on them both: 1) Remaining in debt is sinful before God; and 2) If we continue to mishandle the worldly wealth God gives us, He will withhold from us the consistent manifestation of the glory of His grace.

May God deliver His people from slavery again.

*These things are discussed in depth in Larry Burkett's book, *Victory Over Debt*. (Chicago: Northfield Publishing, 1992)

Spiritual Gifts

There are different kinds of gifts, but the same Spirit. There are different kinds of service, but the same Lord. There are different kinds of working, but the same God works all of them in all men.
—1 Corinthians 12:4-6

John Wesley was used of God in the 18th Century to ignite a movement in the British Isles that now spans the entire globe. This impact of this movement is unparalleled in modern history. When asked about the how he impacted so many in his day, Wesley replied, "I set myself on fire and people come to watch me burn."

This is how I believe God wants us to use our gifts for Him. God wants us to use them with FIRE. The gifts of God that we have are from the Spirit of God. We must discern what our gifts from God are and SET ourselves ON FIRE IN them.

We set a fire and keep a fire when we realize the grace that God has given us and we straightway give it away. If God gives you a revelation in the Scriptures that you know is sound and mature, give it away. If God gives you money, set aside your tithe and, if possible, an additional offering and pass it on. If God wakes you up with a song, DO NOT BE ASHAMED TO SING IT. Whatever God gives you, OPEN YOUR EYES, find that somebody—anybody—that needs it and give it away. A fire works by consuming what it is given and passing it on in power, heat and light. LET THE FIRE BURN.

See God's great gifts to you today. Consume them in your holy fire and give them away. Be encouraged.

Remember the Lord

But remember the Lord your God, for it is he who gives you the ability to produce wealth, and so confirms his covenant, which he swore to your forefathers, as it is today. —Deuteronomy 8:18

The key to managing personal finances is remembrance. God wants us to remember Him and focus on Him as source and giver of all things. He also wants us to be responsible to Him for what He has given. (Matt. 25:14-29)

There is a blessing in remembering and a curse in not remembering God in our financial stewardship. The blessing is this: when we remember the Lord and focus on Him, we have a consistent recognition that all our needs are met. As a steward, though we only may have charge over a small plot, we have the resources of the whole kingdom behind us in support.

The curse in not remembering God is twofold. First, we have to worry about someday not having enough. We have to hoard our resources and seek after vain material wealth just to have security. Second, God is displeased with our attitude of "using" Him just to get what we want. When we neglect to trust Him for all things, we always find ourselves running into the brick wall of our own limitations.

As stewards of God's blessings, we can call upon Him to direct us and assist us in causing His possession to grow and expand. Remembering God and acknowledging His ownership of all that we have places the things squarely on His shoulders and not ours. For your success in life and your peace and mind, I encourage you to remember.

Stewardship

The earth is the LORD's, and everything in it, the world, and all who live in it.
—Psalm 24:1

What are your life goals? Do they include goals for personal wealth? Is there a burning desire for amassing more and more money? The fact is, in our society we extremely overemphasize making more money.

Consider Adam. In the beginning, he possessed the whole earth for God. He named every animal and had charge over every living creature that moved on the earth. Adam had prosperity and position in a perfect world—all the world tells us we should want and seek after. Yet, God looked at Adam and said for the first time in the Biblical account of creation, "Not good."

When we seek so earnestly to increase our possessions, our standing, our "net worth," we fall drastically behind in what is really important. Hear the wisdom of the Scriptures: "A good name is more desirable than great riches; to be esteemed is better than silver or gold" (Prov. 22:1); "What does it profit a man to gain the whole world and lose his own soul" (Luke 9:25, KJV); "The blessing of the Lord maketh rich, and he adds no sorrow to it." (Prov. 10:22, KJV)

It is so much better to focus on God and what He

feels important. He is the possessor of the earth and all it contains; He will give us all that we need in our time of need if we seek Him. I thank God that He has only made us stewards of His possessions, because ownership would kill us.

Be encouraged.

A Burning Bush

The Light of Israel will become a fire, their Holy One a flame; in a single day it will burn and consume his thorns and his briers. —Isaiah 10:17

There are many of us that have an encounter with God—a "burning bush" experience, if you will. It is wonderful to sense and feel the manifest presence of the Most High in our midst. What we must do, however, is to avoid trivializing this experience, glorying so much in it that we miss the greater point.

Beloved, we are a people who love to dance around the burning bush. However, God wants to take us higher. God wants to take us into realms of glory we cannot now imagine. Consider Enoch. The Bible suggests he diligently sought God. He got so close, God did not allow death to take him. Think on Paul. This man gave of himself for more than thirty years of his life, embraced poverty and ridicule with gladness, and committed himself to Christ. God in turn took him in the spirit to the third heaven where His Great Throne is set to behold things unspeakable. Again, think on John. Stoned; tortured; exiled and ridiculed; John suffered more than can be imagined, but he was so close to God that God showed him such a powerful revelation for the church that anyone that adds to or takes away any words from it face damnation before God.

December 30

God wants to take us into the fearful places—the places where His glory becomes so wonderful, it is dangerous. He does not pick and choose some to go and others not to go; God, the great God of heaven, is making His will known: He wants all of us to come to Him.

Pure Hearts

Grieve, mourn and wail. Change your laughter to mourning and your joy to gloom. —James 4:9

Let your heart be convicted this day for its resistance to the Spirit! Suppress not the weeping and mourning that arises in your heart (see John 16:20-22). God must burn away your thorns and briers. God must cause your heart to forsake your personal privilege and desire. God must cripple your willfulness as He crippled Jacob and gave him a new walk to fit his new name.

How I encourage you, beloved, to press into the fire of God. Press into it and be freed from your love of the world. Love God with your whole heart. God longs to be with us truly and to shows us the great riches of His glory in Christ Jesus (Eph. 1:17-18).

Printed in the United States
1316700001BA/34-228